RAMBLER

A Family Pushes Through the Fog of Mental Illness

Linda K. Schmitmeyer

For information, please address:
The Artists' Orchard, LLC
P.O. Box 113593
Pittsburgh, PA 15241

www.theartistsorchard.com

ISBN: 978-0-9964592-5-9

Library of Congress Control Number: 2018945479

Produced in the United States of America

Dedication

To Steve, whose magnanimous nature
made writing this book possible. And to
Nancy, who was with me through every
step of the journey.

Preface

Some things are slow to ripen. Pineapple and pears. Perception and understanding.

The story I share in *Rambler: A Family Pushes Through the Fog of Mental Illness* was slow to ripen, in part because of external circumstances. After the tumultuous decade in which my husband's mental health problems surfaced and resettled into a manageable routine, there were children to care for, money to earn, and an evolving chronic illness to take in and manage.

But there were also internal forces to reckon with. When my husband, Steve, emerged from the shadow of his illness, I was exhausted. Too worn down to think about writing a book, even though I kept a journal with an eye toward sharing the experience with others. And I was angry. Angry that the trajectory of my life changed. That responsibility for our family fell to me. That life dreams faded.

Steve was stable, yes, but different from the person he'd been. Happy and easy-going again, but no longer the life partner he once was. In many ways, I became a caregiver, monitoring his health and managing his life. Understanding and adapting to a new way of being together took time.

I clearly remember the moment I understood the extent to which Steve's illness had changed our life. It was an epiphany of sorts, a point in time when I knew that we'd never return to the way we'd been. That going forward, I would have to rethink my life and build anew. It was a Friday evening in early January, a year after a psychiatrist finally found the cocktail of medications that quieted Steve's mind.

I'd just gotten home from my job at the newspaper and was standing at the kitchen sink, fixing a special dinner for my forty-ninth birthday. There'd been a time when my birthdays were more celebratory, when we went to a restaurant as a family or Steve and I saw a play in Pittsburgh. But that evening, I was waiting for him to get home from the first day of his new job. He was a mechanical engineer prior to his illness, and he'd recently found part-time work in the hardware department at Sears. By this time our three children were older— between the ages of nine and nineteen— and the walking-on-eggshell feeling that I experienced through much of our crisis was passing; I was beginning to trust that we'd weathered the storm.

I heard Steve's Rambler pull into the driveway, but waited inside, not wanting to appear too anxious. Although he'd worked off and on through the acute stage of his illness, his efforts weren't all that successful. There was a lot riding on this job because I knew how desperately he wanted to work. It would help ease family finances, but, more importantly, it was essential for him in regaining a sense of well-being.

When he walked through the front door, I knew immediately that he'd had a good day. His face was alight with a smile. Returning to work was another step closer to where he wanted to be. For a moment, I was happy.

But, as often happened then, darker thoughts clouded my happier ones. Instead of lingering on Steve's smile, my eyes drifted downward to the red Sears vest he was wearing. On the right breast pocket, below the company logo, dangled a white ribbon that read, "In Training." Seeing it, I was overcome with feelings of loss. "When will it stop hurting?" I wrote in my journal. "Why does every step towards regaining a normal life have to be a reminder of what has been lost?"

I needed time to heal before sharing this story. To process what happened; to think and feel; to grieve and reimagine. I did that by writing this book. For more than a decade, I squirreled myself away in the local library and, through writing, explored the many facets of our experience: How did having young children in the home complicate the situation? What role did Steve's and my upbringing play in dealing with our challenge? When did I learn to trust my instincts in responding to Steve when his symptoms flared? How critical was the support of others in overcoming an illness that people didn't talk about openly? Why did our marriage survive and thrive, when so many others fail? How are our children different in their adult life for having gone through this experience? How are Steve and I different?

With time, I began to answer those questions, ostensibly for others who one day may be looking for support in understanding their own challenge. Although I thought of this book as a way of offering insight into the complex and confusing nature of mental illness, writing it proved far more important to my own well-being. Thinking about our experience forced me to look inward, and in doing so, I gained a better understanding of what happened—and of myself. Writing this book gave me a deeper appreciation for the intersecting communities in which we live—families, neighborhoods, schools, hometowns, the workplace—and for the resiliency of the human spirit.

I share *Rambler* now, with enhanced understanding and perspective. I hope it captures our family's experience—not the clinical, analytical construct that the medical profession must deal with, but one that many people live through every day.

RAMBLER

A Family Pushes Through the Fog of Mental Illness

Chapter 1

Despair

Getting home late from my job at the newspaper, I pause at the front door. The growing darkness hides me from my family. Work was difficult, and I am tired. My arrival always sets my family's evening in motion, and I'm not ready for that yet. Cooking dinner and supervising homework. Packing lunches and overseeing bedtimes. John, a high school senior, has ice hockey practice tonight. He's the team captain and likes to be at the rink early. Because I'm late, he'll miss the family meal, a tradition I cling to despite the upheaval of the past several years. Standing there, I see John framed in one of the narrow windows that flank our front door. He sits in a tiny island of light in the living room doing homework, his long legs stretched out between the black wrought-iron frame of an antique school desk. The oldest of my three children, John has been studying at that desk since he was eight. That's when I refinished it and created a personal study space for him. A former high school English teacher, I wanted an organized, well-lighted study area for each of my children. But John is the only one who uses his desk to do homework. Luke, four years younger, sprawls on his bed the few times a week he studies. His vintage desk, crammed in a corner of his bedroom, is piled high with well-thumbed dirt bike magazines.

Eight-year-old Elly does her homework at the island counter in the kitchen; her school desk, in a corner by the back door, serves as a storehouse for her markers, crayons, and artwork. Taped on the wall behind her desk are several of her drawings depicting our family—a smiling mom and dad, two older brothers, herself, and the family pets: Spot, our two-year-old Jack Russell Terrier; Gray Girl, one of the friendlier barn cats that hangs out at the back door for a handout;

and a round glass bowl of nameless goldfish. Arcing across her blue-crayoned skies are colorful rainbows and bright balls of sunshine. On one of the drawings she's written a line from a Shel Silverstein poem: "Welcome to the land of happy." Elly's drawings reflect the indomitable spirit of a child, but they remind me of what's been lost.

Through the other narrow window I see my husband of twenty-two years milling about the kitchen. "Don't let this be a hard night," I murmur when Steve comes into view. Since the onset of his mental health problems several years ago, I've taken to whispering to myself. It's my way of summoning strength from forces beyond my knowing. These entreaties help me feel part of something greater than myself, connected to a power that can control things in a way I no longer can. I feel vulnerable tonight, fearful that simple family responsibilities will be too much for my weakening resolve. It's March of 1997, and for too long I have been living with the fallout from Steve's bipolar disorder. Tonight I worry how much more I can take.

John looks up as I open the door and step inside. His eyes dart to the center of the living room, and my gaze follows to a dozen seat belts draped neatly over the backs of the upholstered furniture. The long, wide belts rest on clean bath towels, their large metal buckles dangling against the backs of the couch and chairs. They're spaced evenly apart, like birds on a telephone wire.

John and my eyes meet and he offers his typical "Hi...iii," a stretched-out syllable that holds my attention long enough for him to gauge my mood. John is well aware of the havoc his father's illness has caused. He was with Steve when he had his initial breakdown at an SAE engineering conference in Detroit more than two years ago. As the oldest, he remembers easier times; he also knows how different things are now. I sigh deeply and turn towards the kitchen.

"Where are Luke and Elly?" I ask Steve, who stands at the island counter, his arms buried to his elbows in a five-gallon bucket of water.

"I don't know," he says flatly. I can see he's fighting to stay focused on cleaning the seat belts. Another five-gallon bucket brims with soap suds on the island counter, the word "wash" scrawled in large black marker on its side. Luke, an eighth-grader, and Elly, a third-grader, are probably parked in front of a TV somewhere. They'll need prodding to start their homework.

"What are you doing?" I ask.

I hear the edge in my voice, but I'm careful not to antagonize him. Once so easy-going, now he flares with anger at the slightest provocation. Since Steve was diagnosed with situational depression, the initial phase of his mental health troubles, my own emotions fluctuate greatly—between anguish at the loss of an active and engaged husband and father and anger at being forced to shoulder so much responsibility. A part-time writing instructor at a community college north of Pittsburgh at the onset of his troubles, I quickly found a job as the features editor for our local newspaper. I only planned working full-time until Steve was able to return to his job as a mechanical engineer. That hasn't happened, and I'm losing faith that it ever will. It's been four years since Steve began taking medication for mood swings. First depression and now bipolar disorder. And the doctors still haven't found a drug combination that will quiet his unstable mind.

Standing in my kitchen, I worry that my words may be a flashpoint for another psychotic episode. My stomach knots at the memory of his furtive leave-takings, when he sneaks away in his Rambler and drives aimlessly through the countryside. When this happens, he thinks people are following him, like they did in Detroit when he was at an engineering society conference. The FBI had him under surveillance there for threatening SAE's executive vice president. On the last day of the conference, when his mind tipped to insanity, the Detroit police took him away in handcuffs. When paranoia flares now, two years after the breakdown, he still thinks people are following him.

"What are you doing with the buckets?" I repeat, careful to soften my voice.

"My Rambler needs a fifth seat belt," says Steve, whose everyday driver is a thirty-year-old Rambler American, a small boxy vehicle that he likes for its "honest" look. He bought his first Rambler more than a dozen years ago, a '59 Classic in excellent condition. But since he's been sick and money is tight, he's acquired—either cheaply or through his car friends—another half-dozen or so less reliable ones, some of which are rusting away behind our barn.

I can see Steve struggle against the distraction. His ability to focus and organize his thoughts has been greatly compromised by his illness. Simple tasks—like picking up a few groceries or calculating the gas mileage for one of his cars—often end in failure. Now he must rely on me to plan his day, remember appointments, and take his medication, even to tell him what day it is.

But he won't need any reminder about washing the seatbelts; that will occupy him for the next several days. It's beyond my understanding how he can fixate on something so peripheral to our

lives while ignoring a house falling down
around him. There was a time when he
could fix anything. Now he rarely tack-
les a home-repair project, and there is
no money to hire someone. I'm hauling
baskets of wet clothes to the Laundro-
mat because the dryer is broken. When a
bathroom faucet leaked, he put a bucket
under the sink. But I'm the one who emp-
ties it. From the dining room window I
can see a small horse-drawn plow leaning
against a tree in the backyard. He used it
a year ago trying to fix a drainage tile. The
plow is still there; the tile is still plugged.
Now, on this early spring evening, he's
preoccupied with washing seat belts in my
kitchen.

"When I went to get a seat belt from
one of the Ramblers, I decided to unbolt
and wash all the belts," he says. "I'm also
cleaning the ones I got from a junkyard."

"Why?" I ask sharply, my voice rising in frustration. "That's almost thirty
seatbelts. You don't need to wash them."

"There's a flea market next week,
and I want to try and sell them," he says.
"I'm oiling the buckles, too, so they work

better."

Steve knows we need money. He's worked only sporadically for the past several years, and he often concocts ways to help out. After the episode in Detroit, the psychiatrist he was seeing at the time reassured me that people with bipolar disorder often return to living normal lives. It's been over two years, and that hasn't happened. Still, I cling to the hope that with the right combination of medications, he'll work again.

Steve returns to what he is doing. His eyes shift from bucket to bucket as he works to re-establish his routine. A cut-off broom handle protrudes from the soapy bucket; he's using it to agitate the belts. There's another bucket for a second washing and a third one for rinsing. A stack of wet belts drips on a sodden bath towel on another counter; a tangled mound of dry ones lie in a heap on the kitchen table.

I open my mouth to protest but see the set of his jaw and the veiled look in his eyes. Nothing I say will make him be the husband and father I need. Turning away, I move to the front door and pause, my hand on the latch, the weight of John's gaze palpable on the nape of my neck. Anger surges in me, and I slip towards despair. How long can I be the rock to which this family clings? I work and I cook and I clean. I take care of the children and worry over money. When psychotic eruptions drive Steve from our home to wander paranoid and dangerously through the countryside, I take control, working with his psychiatrist to get him the medical attention he needs. And when bad dreams drive Elly from her bed at night, I tell her to breathe deeply. Lying in the darkness beside her, I rub her back and stroke her fine blonde hair, soothing fears she doesn't understand. When her breath evens and she drifts into a child's sleep, tears well in my eyes. How will this struggle play out in the lives of my children? John will leave for college soon. Will he ever want to come home? And then I remember Luke, his face contorted in anger as he accused me of making excuses about his father's outbursts as symptoms of an illness, then punishing Luke for his own lack of restraint. "He could control himself if he wanted to," Luke yelled, the blue vein in his neck swelling with rage. "If you put a gun to his head, he could control himself."

"No he can't," I told Luke, who struggles to make sense of an illness that affects the core of his father's being. I also say this to quiet my own doubts about an illness that challenges deeply held beliefs about the personal control we have over our lives. I've always believed that by fixing your mind to a task, you can do anything. People should be able to control their thoughts and actions. Now I'm struggling to understand my husband's mind, which rarely sees things as I do now.

Standing at the front door, my hand resting on the latch, I feel John watching me. He cannot hold me tonight, nor can my cursed sense of responsibility keep me in this hellhole. I throw open the door and walk out.

Chapter 2

The Sandy-Haired Skater

A small fire burns in a fifty-five-gallon oil drum at the edge of an open-air ice-skating rink. It's the fall of 1972, and I am in my senior year at the University of Dayton, a Catholic college forty miles south of the small Ohio manufacturing town where I grew up. I'm standing by the fire with my sister, Nancy, a junior at the university. I am studying literature and history to be a teacher after I graduate. Nancy likes science and math and will become a physical therapist. Steve is also at the rink, and Nancy and I watch as he pulls a group of skaters in a round of crack the whip.

Nancy and I don't usually spend our Saturday evenings together, or any other time on campus either. Our bond

will strengthen in the years ahead, when
I turn to her for support. Now we go our
separate ways. She and her friends are
here because her boyfriend's fraternity is
sponsoring the event. I came because it's
something different from my usual Saturday night wandering between parties
in what UD students call The Ghetto, a
housing area adjacent to campus where
upper-class students live. As we watch
Steve and his friends on the ice, we warm
ourselves by the fire, both of us mellow
from the swig of booze we drank from the
wineskin Steve has hanging around his
neck.

My college friends include many
from Marycrest Hall, the dorm for
freshman and sophomore women. On
a knoll at the upper end of campus,
Marycrest is a newer building; it houses
the surge of baby-boomers who've entered
college recently. Red brick with sleek
aluminum window frames, it contrasts
sharply to the more stately buildings at
the other end of campus. The freshman
and sophomore boys live in a separate
dorm but eat their meals at Marycrest.

That's where I was first introduced to Steve. It was our freshman year, and I was sitting in the lobby with a friend waiting for others to join us before going through the cafeteria line. Steve and I were among the many eighteen-year-olds from towns and farming communities north of Dayton who congregated in the lobby that first year, drawn by our common heritage—German, Catholic, and working class, whose family trees often overlapped at the edges. One of Steve's and my earliest conversations was about Wally Post, the star right fielder for the Cincinnati Redlegs when we were in grade school. He was a sports hero who grew up in a crossroads community near our hometowns. We both boasted of being related: Steve's grandmother was a Post, and my mother always said she was Wally's second cousin.

The older of two girls in a family with ten boys—I'm fifth and Nancy is sixth in birth order—I was born in 1950, shortly after my parents moved into the first and only home they ever owned. They rented through the first eight years of

their marriage, in part because my father
was in the army, stationed as a cook at a
base in San Diego for the duration of the
war. But by 1950, with a fifth child on
the way, they needed a bigger house. It
was a boxy, white-framed two-story with a
big back yard. We kids spent a lot of time
there, playing pick-up games of baseball.
When my ninth brother, Joe, was born,
people said we had a ready-made baseball
team. In fact, we had a team before then,
because Nancy was as good at baseball as
some of my older brothers. The younger
boys were always picked last, and I was
relegated to cheer from the sidelines. Unless Mom intervened. She always kept a
watchful eye on our backyard activities
from the kitchen window. If she didn't like
what she saw, she'd crank the window
open wide enough for her naturally soft
voice to project over the noise. "Everyone
gets to play," she'd say, and, reluctantly,
all of us were allowed into the game.

I preferred indoor games, though,
playing house and schoolteacher with
whatever little brothers I could pull into
my fantasy. I also loved reading. On Sat-

urday mornings, Nancy and I walked the mile to our public library for a week's supply of books—Nancy Drew mysteries, *Little Women*, *Old Yeller*, *The Three Faces of Eve*. Walking slowly home with my nose in a book, I usually finished the first one before I got there. I was a dreamy child, and books offered a peek into the lives of people and places more thrilling than those around me. It also helped moderate the mild melancholia I often felt as a child, a kind of slow sadness unbeknown to others and, when I was younger, even unto myself. It was mostly a feeling of separateness, of being on the outside looking in. Surrounded by many, I often was lonely. Reading helped ease the ordinariness I felt growing up. Sober thoughts for one whose upbringing didn't encourage exploring life's darker emotions.

Childrearing in a family with lots of kids—at least in our family—meant everything was done in batches, whether being read bedtime stories or sharing a bathtub. I liken it to Mom preparing the family meal: a kind of mass production that didn't take individual differences

into account. With emotional sensibili-
ties that sometimes felt overlooked, I often
longed for recognition that wasn't there.
From these melancholic childhood experiences emerged a propensity for looking
inward, not just towards myself, although
I did that, but also at the subtle, often
silent interplay of others. While not overly
drawn to being with people, I love watching them live their lives.

These childhood experiences were
instrumental in developing an inner discipline that helped me through the difficult
years with Steve. Early on I learned that a
family's well-being superseded the needs
and wants of the individual. My childhood
also served as a foundation for appreciat-
ing the deeper contentment that is found
in pursuing life's larger purposes, instead
of one's personal interests. Life lessons a
child is slow to comprehend.

● ● ●

I wasn't always sure I'd be allowed
to go to college. My father worked as a
baker and my mother was at home. To-

gether they were ingenious in providing for their large brood on my father's meager salary, but paying for college was well beyond their means. Although Mom and Dad rarely talked openly about money, it was an underlying tension in our home—one that broke the surface when a brother hit a baseball through a window or one of us spilled milk at the supper table. With so many arms reaching for food, that happened a lot. First came Dad's anger, as Mom quickly lifted the plastic tablecloth to contain the spill. After the cleanup, he simmered in silence for the remainder of the meal.

"Why do you want to go to college?" Dad asked when I first began thinking about life beyond high school. He'd just gotten home from the restaurant where he worked, and I was upstairs in the girls' bedroom, a small pink-and-white room I shared with Nancy. My brothers slept in two of the four bedrooms, and my parents in a large room at the front of the house, one shaded by an elm tree that grew in the yard. I was surprised to see Dad framed in my bedroom door; it was unusual for him to initiate conversations like that. The stickier issues of raising children were left to Mom, who somehow managed to stay on top of each of her children's increasingly complex lives.

Usually after a brief rest on the living room couch, Dad headed to his basement workshop before supper, or to one of the several gardens he maintained throughout our hometown. The evening meal was a sacrosanct event in our home, and each night we gathered around the big dining room table with washed hands. Prayers were said and food was passed clockwise, with Mom keeping a watchful eye on the portion of meat each of us took. Looking back, the memorable part of these meals was afterwards, when we sat around the table talking. Dad often shared what he'd read in the newspaper or something he'd heard at work. When I was in high school, I remember him telling us about a radar range that had been installed at the restaurant. It can cook food in a matter of seconds, he'd said.

And Mom, attuned to the minutia of her children's lives, often asked us about our day. What books we got from the library or how we did on a particular test at school.

To my father, who grew up during the Depression and quit school after the eighth grade, going to college must have seemed an unnecessary extravagance for a daughter who, as he put it, "would probably get married and have children." I was propped up against the headboard doing homework when he said this, listening to my radio. It was a sleek-looking Motorola with lots of chrome; I bought it with my first paycheck from the grocery store where I worked. I especially liked how it contrasted to our home's well-worn furnishings. All of us kids got jobs when we turned sixteen. I'd been allowed to spend my first paycheck as I wanted, so I bought the radio. After that, half of what I earned went to Mom for household expenses.

I wasn't taken aback by my father's comment; in fact, it was reflective of the time and place in which I grew up. Few of the fifty-three students in my high school graduating class went on to college, especially the girls. Most of my classmates found work in offices and factories or joined the military. I'd been dating the same young man since I was a sopho- more, so my father's assumption about marrying my high school sweetheart didn't seem unreasonable.

"Dan and Bob went away to col- lege," I said, referring to two of my broth- ers who left home after high school, Dan to the University of Dayton, and Bob to a school in Boston where he studied for a year to become an African missionary, after which he transferred to UD. My two other older brothers, Bill and John, joined the Navy. "I want to go away to school too."

"You know your mother and I can't help you pay for it," he said.

"I know," I answered.

At eighteen, I didn't have a realistic plan about paying for college, other than I would apply for scholarships and grants like my brothers. I also had no idea what I wanted to do with my life, other than to leave home like them. There had to be something more exciting than the life I was living, and college seemed like a fun way to make that happen.

• • •

Standing by the fire with Nancy at the ice rink, I think back to that conversation with my father. I will graduate from college soon with a clearer sense of what I want to do with my life. After graduation, I will be a high school English teacher. I will have my own apartment, and during my summer vacations—in the three years before Steve and I marry—I will travel to the places I read about in books. I will crisscross North America in my Volkswagen van, sleeping on beaches in Malibu and under the stars of Vancouver Island. I will hike the Rockies and smoke pot at a fiddlers' convention in Nova Scotia. I may not have known what I wanted when I left home four years ago, but I do now.

Pulled from my musings by Steve skating fast towards us, I watch as he slices the ice and stops within inches of us. The fire barrel hisses. Although Steve and I met as freshman, we haven't talked much, only brief hellos when we see each other on campus. Raising the wineskin over his head, he offers Nancy and me another swig of whiskey. We talk for a while, and soon he returns to the ice. Again Steve motions the skaters to fall in line for crack the whip. He's a strong skater, a skill he acquired playing ice hockey on a lake near his family's farm. The oldest of three children and the only son of a dairy farmer, Steve grew up about twenty minutes from my hometown. His family farmed land near there since the 1830s, when his great-great grandfather emigrated from Germany. But Steve isn't interested in taking over the farm. When he graduates next year, he will take a job as a mechanical engineer at Wright-Patterson Air Force Base in Dayton.

Warmed by the fire and the booze, I watch Steve glide gracefully across the ice, his easy smile and open countenance an invitation for others to join him. With a string of skaters behind him, he leans forward, digging his old hockey skates into the ice until he has sufficient momentum. Then he turns sharply, whipping them across the ice.

When the chain reassembles, Nancy and I scramble to reach the back of the line. Although Nancy outshone me in backyard baseball, I hold my own on the ice and take my place at the end of line. The chain begins to move, and we zigzag in wide swooping motions. When Steve turns, the skaters' outstretched arms brace against the energy moving down the chain. When the charge reaches me, I hold tight for a while, then lose my grip and fly wildly across the ice. I wobble, then land in a heap at the far end of the rink.

Shaking off the fall, I look up and see Steve watching me, his head tilted back in laughter. He skates quickly towards me, showering me with ice when he stops. Extending his hand, he smiles brightly down at me. Although I've known Steve casually for several years, it feels like I am seeing him for the first time—a tall, thin sandy-haired skater with a brilliant smile.

• • •

Several months later, I am sitting on the front stoop of my house in UD's ghetto, waiting for Steve to pass by. It is an unusually warm day in early spring, and by this time I know his class schedule well enough to be outside when he walks by. He joins me on the stoop, and we sit together talking. It's still early in our dating relationship, and we haven't shared many thoughts or feelings yet. But I'm itching to know more about this highly energetic and happy-go-lucky man; I probe a little deeper.

"You're always so upbeat," I say. "Don't you ever feel low?"

Steve seems puzzled, unsure of what I'm asking.

I've had several serious boyfriends in high school and college, but no one as much fun as Steve. He has a natural exuberance that draws others to him, but also from whom he derives his inner charge. Instead of traditional Saturday night movie dates at the student union, Steve likes more adventuresome outings. Sledding on cafeteria trays down Stuart Hill or wandering a nearby cemetery at night. He's taught me to snow ski at a small resort south of Dayton and water ski behind his father's fishing boat. He's as skillful at skiing as he is at skating, and a very patient teacher.

But Steve hasn't been in a long-term relationship before, and I can see that he isn't use to these kinds of questions.

"You know. Don't you ever get down? Are you ever depressed?"

"Depressed?" He pauses, puzzled by the concept.

"By life," I say. "By how hard things can be. Anything. Don't you ever feel sad?"

"I really have nothing to feel sad about," Steve says.

"Really?" I say. Now it's my turn to be confused. Are there people who aren't subjected to the everyday sadness that lingers in the shadows of our life?

"I like most everything I do," he says. "I have good friends, and I get along well with my parents. Studying is hard, but worth it. I've wanted to be an engineer ever since my sixth-grade science teacher told me I'd be good at it."

He pauses a moment longer, then says, "The only time I ever felt down was when a friend broke a window on my new Porsche." He then tells me how his friend cracked the vent window when pulling himself from the low-riding two-seater, an early college graduation present Steve and his parents purchased together.

I laugh out loud. His explanation seems a glib response to my probing question, but I can see he is sincere. Is this man immune from the highs and lows that afflict most of us? I am intrigued by Steve's boundless exuberance and emotional evenness; it is an appealing contrast to my more sober self.

Chapter 3

Gray Matters

If disease and disorders were coded by color, then gray would best represent mental illnesses: Achromatic, the color of smoke; where black and white overlap, where health and sickness intersect. Steve's manic depression, as it was called in the early-1990s, didn't manifest in any medically discernable manner, like a lump on a breast or an elevated PSA number. Instead, it crept into our family life over a period of several years, an indefinable force that disrupted routines and changed our lives without our knowing it was happening.

I never thought of Steve's quickening temper as a symptom of an illness; I blamed it on the stress of several job changes during a short period of time and the pressure of providing for our growing family. Add to that the large financial loss we sustained selling our eighty-acre farm when we moved from Ohio to Pennsylvania when Steve changed jobs. There was no Internet to search or television advertisements to advise me that Steve's irritability may be the sign of a mental disorder. Nor any biological marker doctors could point to. I saw only slight changes in his personality and thinking, which I attributed to the financial pressures we faced. Gradually Steve's sleep became erratic, his mood more volatile. Established patterns reinforced by our fifteen years together began to erode: Family meals—as important to me as they had been to my mother—were no longer assured. Steve, preoccupied and agitated, didn't always join us. And when he did, he sometimes turned irritable, upsetting everyone.

Then, as suddenly as his anger surfaced, it ended, and the Steve of earlier times was there, laughing and interacting with the children as he once did, leaving me to wonder if it was my perceptions that had been distorted by stress.

Throughout those in-between years—from the day Steve walked into the kitchen after work one day and told me that he'd quit his job until a full-blown psychotic breakdown five years later—Steve's shifting moods and behaviors created a palpable tension in our home. Without consciously doing so, our family had slipped into a walking-on-eggshells existence, where a word or action triggered a quarrel that spiraled uncharacteristically out of control. Mostly, though, the family's internal harmony—the unacknowledged peacefulness that had been part of our earlier life—had disappeared.

• • •

After graduating from the University of Dayton, Steve worked for fourteen years at Wright-Patterson monitoring government contractors who developed ground-support equipment for military aircraft. He liked it there, earning a patent for a mechanical system he and a coworker designed that prevented helicopter hoist cables from tangling when retracting. With time, though, Steve grew tired of the bureaucracy, where politics played a role in technical decisions and promotions were sometimes based on your degrees instead of the work you did. Steve had enrolled in a master's degree program for several semesters shortly after he began working at Wright-Patterson, but classroom learning had never been easy for him. After a while, he was itching for a change. It came in his mid-thirties, through SAE International, a professional society for automotive and aerospace engineers. SAE offered him a job at its headquarters north of Pittsburgh, where he would oversee committees that developed technical standards for the aerospace industry.

Steve's job change meant moving our young family and a barn full of farm machinery to Pennsylvania. Although Steve was never interested in following his family's farming tradition, he loved old farm equipment. We'd bought an 1840s farmhouse a half hour north of Dayton when we first married. It had three outbuildings where he stored the antique farm equipment he'd begun collecting. By the time we moved to Pennsylvania, he'd acquired an antique wagon and manure spreader, several full-size farm tractors and a number of garden tractors, and an old Checker Cab. That's not farm equipment, but he once hauled a sheep buck to market in it. And to make it more farm-like, he painted the cab body John Deere green and the wheels John Deere yellow. Most treasured among Steve's collection was the '51 Ferguson tractor he'd inherited when his parents sold the dairy farm. It's the tractor Steve learned to drive on when he was only five years old.

We bought a newer home on ten acres when we moved to Pennsylvania, a stone and cedar two-story tucked into a hillside. Our house, where we still live, is situated half way down a steep hill, about a hundred yards from a winding country road. The back of the house has lots of big windows and overlooks a century-old barn, a fenced pasture, and several acres of woods. At the far end of the property, at the bottom of the long sloping hill, is a small pond. The home was a great place to raise a family. John, who was seven when we moved there, inherited a small Kawasaki dirt bike that belonged to the previous owner's son. It was the first of many motorized vehicles that Steve and the kids raced around our property.

Steve and I were excited about living someplace new, even though the move wasn't easy. Farmland prices had depreciated since we'd bought the Ohio farm, and we lost a great deal of money when we sold it. Steve also started working at SAE six months before we moved. And the move itself was difficult; it involved transporting several of Steve's full-size tractors and other antique farm equipment as well as a goat, a pet rooster, several geese, a barn cat and her kittens, and our dog. By the time we settled in to our new home, though, we'd put the challenges of the year behind us and were excited about our new life in Pennsylvania.

• • •

Sitting at the kitchen table with the boys as they eat an after-school snack, I hear Steve's car pull into the driveway.

We've been in our new home for three years now, and the easy rhythm of our daily life has returned. Steve is home from work earlier than usual, which means he probably has to catch a flight tomorrow morning. When that happens, he tries to be home shortly after the boys get off the school bus. John is in the fourth grade at the local public school, and Luke, six, is in his third year of a Montessori preschool program. Elly, born two years after our move to Pennsylvania, is almost one. She sits in her high chair, happy to have her brothers nearby.

I can see Steve through the kitchen window. He's crossing the cement pad that he and his father poured when we first moved here. At forty, Steve is still slender and fit, with only hints of gray in his sandy blonde hair. He's wearing his dark blue suit; a red-striped tie hangs loose around his neck. From afar, he looks like a successful businessman at the end of a workday. I like to tease that he's still a farm boy up close, with his big hands and easy smile. Today, though, his face is drawn. He looks tired and anxious, preoccupied. A rarity in the man I've known for almost twenty years.

Walking into the kitchen, he blurts—while the kids munch on pretzels and carrot sticks: "I quit my job." I'm stunned. Shaking my head, I try to make sense of what I am hearing. Later, out of earshot of the children, he tells me what happened.

"I was talking to my boss about the aerospace conference," Steve says. Steve's boss, who recently joined SAE, is less technical than Steve likes, but together they are organizing a first-ever aerospace conference at Wright-Patterson. Steve had been asked to take the assignment because of his connections at the Air Force base. Planning it involves less technical work than Steve is accustomed to; he often refers to it as "glorified party planning."

"We were talking about a problem with the conference," Steve says. "Nothing out of the ordinary, just another thing we didn't agree on. Right in the middle of the conversation he asked me if I thought SAE was a good fit for me.

"He was friendly," Steve continues, "as if he knew I preferred working aerospace standards to planning a conference. He didn't sound like someone who was going to fire me. I thought maybe he was just trying to get to know me better. I told him that I liked working for SAE. That I wouldn't have sold a farm and moved my family to Pennsylvania if I didn't."

Like everything in Steve's life, he has an over-the-top enthusiasm for SAE. He'd joined the student chapter while at the University of Dayton. As a senior in college, he participated in the engineering society's inaugural student-design competition in Detroit. Teams from different universities competed to design and build small urban vehicles that year. The UD team won an award for its bumper design and placed fairly well overall. The experience permanently sealed Steve's interest in the engineering society, and he quickly became a loyal supporter. He joined SAE's Dayton chapter after graduating from UD and served as Wright-Patterson's area representative. He held several leadership positions in the Dayton chapter and was on track to be chapter president the year we moved to Pennsylvania.

The year before hiring Steve, SAE International honored him as one of three Outstanding Young Engineers. Steve and I traveled to Pittsburgh to receive the award at the society's annual leadership development workshop, which sparked Steve's interest in working for SAE.

"We continued talking," Steve says, "but I could see that something was on his mind." Never one to dance around an issue, Steve questioned his boss outright: "I asked him if he thought I should quit my job at SAE? His lower lip quivered, but he didn't say a word," Steve explains. "And when he didn't say anything, I said, 'Fine.' Then I slapped his desk and said, 'I'm out of here.'"

• • •

In the end, Steve's departure from SAE was amicable. Several days after storming out of his boss' office, he met with human resources, who urged him to

finish his work on the Wright-Patterson
conference before leaving; in exchange,
SAE offered him unemployment benefits
while he looked for another job. When he
finally departed six weeks later, Steve was
happy to be moving on. Buoyed by almost
twenty years of gainful employment, he
was confident he would find another job
and everything would be okay.

My ire over the irresponsible way
in which he left SAE was short-lived;
Steve had always come through for us,
and I expected he would again. I was accustomed to life proceeding as I wanted,
believing that together our determination
and strong work ethic made us immune
to calamity.

Steve found another job in a matter
of weeks, as an engineer at a small ma-
chine shop. That didn't last, though. Six
months later he was laid off. Another job
followed that one, which ended after four
months. Then a college friend asked him
to be a technical sales rep for his company, Plasquip, which sold injection-molding
machines. The plastics industry was
thriving throughout western Pennsylvania

and upstate New York in the early 1990s, but by the end of the decade, most of the operations would be moved overseas. Steve's sales territory covered southwestern Pennsylvania, and he worked from an office we set up on the lower level of our home.

Steve had been hired for three jobs in eighteen months, all new positions created specifically for him. Steve still had the energy and enthusiasm to inspire others in his abilities, but he no longer seemed capable of following through. We blamed his work troubles on downturns in the economy, which was partially true, but I wondered if other factors were involved.

In the following years I thought frequently about why Steve left SAE without having another job lined up. We were only three years into a new mortgage and had three young children. Although Steve was naturally impulsive in his approach to many things, he wasn't irresponsible. He'd spent almost a year looking for the right job before leaving Wright-Patterson. Yet he left SAE on a whim: "I wanted out of there so bad," he'd said. "It happened so fast, but I knew I didn't want to go back."

Steve's technical intelligence and natural enthusiasm for everything mechanical had served him well whenever he faced problems at work. He also was well-liked and respected professionally, especially at the Air Force base. When one of the higher ups learned of his decision to take the SAE job, he suggested that if Steve stayed, he'd be promoted. At Wright-Patterson, his job involved solving technical problems, and he was highly capable of doing that. At SAE, his work centered on achieving consensus for industry standards among the aerospace companies who designed and built airplanes. That required managing complex human interactions, and Steve had never been skillful at understanding people's motives or decoding emotional nuance. He tended to be overtly honest and forthright in his dealings with people, and he assumed others did the same. In retrospect, the political wrangling required to do the kind of work he was doing may have overwhelmed him, something his boss at SAE might have sensed when he asked Steve if he thought SAE was a good fit.

Why he left SAE so abruptly remained unresolved in my mind for a long time; a clearer understanding emerged years later, when the medical community better understood the long-term repercussions of head injuries.

Six months before walking out of his boss' office, Steve sustained a serious concussion. At the time, we were celebrating John's tenth birthday at a BMX park, a dirt track where kids race their bicycles through a series of jumps. When we arrived at the track, John quickly donned his helmet and headed towards the first jump. Seeing John on his bike, Steve grabbed another bicycle and raced after him. He wasn't wearing a helmet. Steve crested the hill and went airborne, as you're supposed to do on a jump. But instead of landing on the rear bike tire, his front tire hit first, causing him to fly over the handlebars. His forehead hit the ground, and he was knocked unconscious for several minutes. Someone called an ambulance, which took him to a Pittsburgh hospital. There he remained cognitively confused until the following morning.

Neither Steve nor I connected the subsequent changes in his thinking and behaviors over the next several years to the bicycle accident. And because Steve's mental health problems emerged gradually—his first visit to a psychiatrist occurred three years after leaving SAE—we never linked the changes in personality to the accident. And when we shared information about Steve's head injury as part of his medical history with the various psychiatrists he saw, they expressed interest and sometimes ordered neurological testing. But this was the mid-1990s, and none of them conclusively connected the bike accident to his mental illness.

Whether the onset of Steve's bipolar disorder was triggered by the concussion is medically unsubstantiated. And in the end, it really didn't matter. Severe mood swings and erratic behaviors are what they are, no matter the cause. At the time,

I was less concerned about why things changed and more focused on how to deal with them.

Later, when medical research about head trauma became more widespread, we linked the changes in Steve's personality to the accident. His abrupt departure from SAE seemed the first instance of recklessness, a behavior change that at times became more pronounced over the next several years. And the increased irritability I thought related to work stress was likely fallout from the concussion. What caused Steve's mental illness remains medically unclear, gray, the color of smoke.

What was clear was that Steve was no longer the gregarious, happy-go-lucky man I married. We were embarking on a period in which outwardly our everyday life appeared as it had once been—Steve working to make a go of Plasquip and me holding tightly to the life I loved—while everything around us fell apart.

Chapter 4

Hanging on to Normal

It's a late October afternoon, two-and-a-half years after Steve quit his job at SAE. Pulling into the driveway from work, I see John and Luke in the garage tinkering with their dirt bikes. Luke, now eight, has inherited John's old Kawasaki, and John bought one more suited for a thirteen-year-old. The two of them and several neighbor boys love riding through the fields and woods behind our houses. John and Luke have their father's mechanical know-how and get along well when bending their heads together over an engine.

• • •

Many of the boys' earliest memories are of motorized play, the first of which was a child's tractor Steve cobbled together from several different garden vehicles. We called it Hunk of Junk, after one of the children's storybooks. Equipped with a 1.5-horsepower engine, the cultivator-turned-tractor traveled less than two miles an hour. John made countless laps with it around the barnyard in Ohio, with two-year-old Luke perched contentedly on the wooden seat Steve added to the back. Hunk of Junk was the first of many riding toys Steve built or adapted for the children. He also jury-rigged a wood blade to the front of a 5-horsepower 1940s garden tractor he bought at an auction; the boys drove it for hours, rearranging the stones in our driveway.

Steve had always been involved in inventing interesting play opportunities for our children, beginning with the set of blocks he made John before we brought him home from the hospital. John was born four years after Steve and I married, in a small, municipal hospital in Ohio. Steve was elated at the idea of being a father, and his enthusiasm spilled over to the others in the undersized delivery room. The head nurse, a middle-aged woman who'd undoubtedly seen many happy fathers, told Steve he was the most enthusiastic father she'd ever seen. Moments after John was born, she fashioned an armband out of medical tape and wrote "Most Excited Dad" on it, then wrapped it around his bicep. And when Steve came to take his new family home, he was holding a long, narrow box of wooden blocks that spelled out: "Hi John, 2 Aug. '79." Too excited to sleep, Steve had stayed up late making the blocks from scrap wood leftover from a home remodeling project.

Before John was a month old, he'd built him a scale-model Jeep pickup. Painted fire engine red, the truck was an interactive toy with which our children would learn basic auto mechanics; the truck's hood was held open with a thick wire, which allowed them to change the four in-line spark plugs. There was a miniature battery, ground wire, and starter, all cooled with a Popsicle-stick radiator fan. Steve even added a tiny wrench to the painted Band-Aid toolbox in the truck bed that they used to change the tires.

Steve's delight in being a parent remained constant as our family grew— Luke was born four years after John, and Elly five-and-a-half years later.

Although Steve was always helpful in caring for the children when they were young, he wasn't necessarily attuned to their everyday needs. Overseeing their daily life fell to me. His strength was in his ability to intuit and cultivate a child's interest. When Luke was a baby, he loved being outdoors, so Steve rigged a five-gallon bucket to the back of an old tractor so he could be with him when working outside. Steve liked having Luke in the bucket while he fed the farm animals or cut firewood. Just a year old, Luke could barely see over the top of the bucket, his little legs protruding from two holes in the base. Luke spent countless hours riding around our farm that way.

Although deeply engaged early on in their play, Steve became more detached after leaving SAE. The boys were older, though, and more capable of working on their dirt bikes without Steve's help. I often found the two of them alone in the garage when I got home from work.

• • •

"Where's your Dad?" I call to John as I lift Elly from her car seat. Three years old, she spends her days at a babysitter down the road from where we live. Steve is all too ready to find an excuse not to call on his Plasquip customers, and I don't want having to watch Elly be one of them.

"I don't know," John says. "He might be sleeping."

"Has he been home long?" I ask, fishing for details about how their father spent his day. When I left this morning, Steve said he was going to call on customers, but his car looks like it hasn't been moved.

"I haven't seen him. His car was here when I got off the bus," says John. "He might be in the office."

After a rocky departure from SAE and the two short-term other jobs, Steve eventually settled into engineering sales for Plasquip. We converted the bedroom on the lower level of our home to an office and furnished it with an antique wooden desk and the family's late-1980s Macintosh. Initially Steve tackled his territory with characteristic enthusiasm and made a number of early sales, but not as many as he'd hoped. After his initial burst of enthusiasm, he became discouraged and began complaining about the solitary nature of working from home. He also had trouble focusing: "I sit at my desk for hours biting my nails," he says. "I just can't concentrate. Time slips away, and I can't figure out where it went."

I work full-time now as a general assignment reporter for a weekly newspaper; I also teach writing two evenings a week at a nearby community college. Initially I thought of the newspaper as a temporary job, a way of carrying the medical benefits until Steve regained his professional footing. It didn't seem long, though, before I was responsible for most everything, especially propping up Steve's flagging morale. Since he left SAE, we've had to sell the two, full-size John Deere tractors we hauled from Ohio. We kept the Fergie to mow pasture and plow the driveway in the winter. It also has sentimental value, since it was the tractor Steve learned to drive on.

I'm also learning how to graciously accept the help of others, extra tickets to a play in Pittsburgh or a quarter of beef from a brother who raises cattle. Knowing how difficult it's gotten, Nancy occasionally sends me a little money to help out, especially around the children's birthdays. Steve seems to withdraw deeper into himself, and his refusal to work harder at making Plasquip successful has created the first real crisis of our marriage.

Heading into the house, I pass the '64 Rambler station wagon that Steve bought sight unseen earlier this year. Before moving to Pennsylvania, he purchased a 1959 Rambler Classic at an auto auction, kicking off what would become an obsession with the conservative, old man's car that lasted through two decades. With less money, though, the '64 Rambler became another point of contention between us. He wanted to replace all our cars with Ramblers, but I wasn't parting with the Pontiac station wagon

I drove. Reluctantly, I agreed to the '64, hoping it would boost his sagging spirit. That is also new in our relationship, me agreeing to things I don't really like just to keep the peace.

Taped in the back window of the '64 is an upside-down bumper sticker he put there; it reads: "Why be normal?" To Steve, the sticker refers to the string of unusual automobiles he's owned, including several '50s-era BMW Isettas, the kind you enter through a door at the front of the car; the John Deere green Checker; a 1950 Plymouth, with its itchy wool seats; and the '59 Rambler he bought at the auction. To me the bumper sticker reflects another ongoing difference between us: He likes oddity, whether in cars or people, and I like normal, or at least the appearance of normalcy.

My reach for affluence—that's how I first defined normalcy—is rooted in my childhood desire to blend in, to be as my friends had been, sons and daughters of working-class families who had and did more things than our family did. My parents struggled to provide us children with the basics, and as a child, I felt our poorness. It was there in the hand-me-down dress I wore for my First Communion, a gift from the Sisters of Charity who taught at the free Catholic school we attended. I also felt it in the imitation Barbie doll I got for my ninth Christmas, instead of a real one like my friends had.

Leaving home at eighteen, I wanted a more interesting life. I was encouraged by a mother who pushed her children to reach beyond their childhood experience. Mom grew up during the Depression, the eldest of eight children of an unsuccessful farmer turned factory worker. Yet Mom's worldview transcended her circumstances. She never allowed herself or her children to think they had fewer opportunities. She pushed us all to do well in school and provided learning experiences within her means: telling stories when doing the weekly ironing, taking us at a young age to the public library, spearheading spontaneous spelling and language games, and making room in our overcrowded home for an exchange student. She was disciplined, determined,

and proud of her intellect; she skipped
a grade when her father moved the family from one farm to another, a story she
liked sharing with her children.

Mom encouraged all of us to go
after what we wanted, and for me, that
meant going away to school (all twelve of
us attended college), becoming a teacher,
traveling, living independently, and marrying the son of a successful dairy farmer
whose family's sense of adventure was
grander than my own family's. Normal
now has come to mean driving a relatively
new automobile, a standard Steve's Ramblers fail to meet.

Although he bought his first Rambler while we lived in Ohio, Steve's preoc-
cupation with these boxy sedans mushroomed throughout the 1990s, coinciding
with the onset of his mental health problems. He'd acquired seven or eight of them
over a half-dozen years, a few working
ones and the others he used as parts
cars. They were relatively inexpensive
compared to the Porsche he drove when
he graduated from college—some free,
others costing less than two grand—yet

sufficiently unusual to satisfy his desire
for a distinctive automobile. They also
had an element of ordinariness that he
relished: "Everybody knows somebody
who's had a Rambler," he said frequently,
his reputation as the man with the old
Ramblers solidified among our family
and friends. He especially liked driving
one when calling on Plasquip customers:
"They can be an ice-breaker when you
meet someone for the first time."

But Steve's Ramblers have become luxuries we can no longer afford.
We've had to give up many of the middle-
class perks we once enjoyed, and I often
think of my mother as I stretch our family's meager income. Despite the strain,
though, Steve bought the Rambler station
wagon. To me it's another reminder of just
how detached he's become from our lives.

● ● ●

Balancing little Elly on my hip, I
pass the Rambler and head inside. Steve
isn't in the home office as I'd hoped. When
I get home I always look for signs to see

whether he's been working at Plasquip.
Instead I find him lying on the floor of our
bedroom, where he often goes when he's
feeling down. It's a habit he picked up
from his father, who rested on the floor
between farm chores because his clothes
were dirty. But Steve is wearing office at-
tire, a short-sleeved dress shirt and tie,
which hangs loose around his neck. He
recently started dressing for work each
morning, even when he didn't have to see
customers. I'd suggested he do so, and he
agreed. He seems to want to do better at
Plasquip, but then always gives up. We
both thought it might help him focus on
his work more, something that's increasingly difficult for him to do.

"Remember we have the Halloween
party tonight," I say, purposefully avoid-
ing any reference to his workday. "I have
to fix dinner and make something to take
to the party. I'm hoping you can pull
together the kids' Halloween costumes.
You're better at that than me."

"Not now," he says flatly. "I want to
rest."

Steve has always been the creative

one when it comes to the kids' Halloween costumes. We rarely purchased them, only a mask or some face paint to enhance whatever costume he makes from things we have around the house. One year he made a costume the kids called "Hunk of Junk," because it held an assortment of spare engine parts. Cutting head- and armholes in a burlap feed sack, he attached pieces of random hardware from the garage: a lawnmower carburetor, barn door hinges, and spark plugs. For a mask they wore the helmet and goggles Steve used when racing his Porsche. After he graduated, Steve joined an autocross club. Participants competed in timed competitions on tracks set up in parking lots. Steve was good at it, one year making it all the way to the nationals.

Another of his Halloween creations was a car made from a cardboard box he painted canary yellow, like the Porsche. He added a steering wheel from his old pedal tractor, an ignition switch, gauges, and a gearshift. He designed another costume to accompany the car, Stop- and Yield-shaped signs cut from cardboard that draped over the boys' shoulders. Of course, John and Luke argued about who got to be the race car and who had to wear the traffic signs.

"Will you do the costumes later?" I ask. "I need your help." I no longer expect anything creative, just something from the previous years' stock stored in the down-stairs mudroom.

"I don't feel like going to the party," he says.

That's another thing Steve does now. He no longer declares his inten-tions outright, but couches his responses in weak language, like "I don't feel" or "I don't think I want to..."

Fearful of an outright "No," I back off, hoping he'll change his mind when it's time to leave. Returning to the kitchen, I work to get ready, driven by seething anger. When I return to the bedroom an hour later, I'm itching for a fight.

"Come with us," I beg. "You can't just lay there all night."

"I don't feel like it," he whines.

"I didn't feel like fixing dinner and making brownies and finding costumes," I

say. "And I didn't feel like working all day.
But I did. You have to make yourself do
things you don't want to do," a refrain I
say often now. "Things don't always come
easy for me, but I make myself do them."

Turning his head away, Steve says
nothing.

Positioning myself so he has to look
at me, I foolishly move the argument from
the party to my default complaint, his
unwillingness—for I still see his apathy as
something he should be able control—to
try harder at Plasquip.

"You don't have to like what you
do," I say. "I know work doesn't excite you
anymore, but, I don't like my job either.
I do it because I have to. We have three
children to care for. You can't just abandon that responsibility."

Steve still doesn't say anything, but
I persevere, returning again to his wasted
day. "You have done nothing today; the
least you can do is go with us," I say. "For
me. For the kids. I don't want to go alone."

Unyielding, Steve buries his face in
the fold of his arms.

Clasping the dresser for balance, I

draw my leg behind me and kick him hard on the bottom of his foot. When he doesn't respond, I kick him again.

A half hour later, the kids and I leave for the party. When we return, Steve is in bed. Diffused of my anger, I lie silently beside him, saddened by my earlier actions and deeply confused by what is happening to us. I awake in the middle of the night and am unable to get back to sleep. Picking up the pen and yellow legal pad I keep by my bed, I begin a letter to Nancy.

After becoming a physical therapist, Nancy married Mark Bokermann, a fellow University of Dayton graduate. They live in northern Illinois, where Mark works in sales for a manufacturing company that makes industrial magnets. They have three sons who mirror our children's ages. Despite the miles between us, our families get together every year for vacation and holidays. Nancy and I talk by phone almost every Sunday, when long-distance rates are low. And as the gulf between Steve and me widens, those weekly phone calls become a way for me to share my

growing concerns about Steve. Together
she and I try to understand what's happening. Other times, when sleep eludes
me, as it does more and more, I write
Nancy a letter, a kind of talk therapy that
helps me fall back to sleep. In an unsent
letter to Nancy that night, I wrote:

> My greatest fear for the past
> year has been Steve losing his
> job again. Little did I know
> that another problem would
> slip to the forefront of our
> lives: Steve's mood, which be-
> comes worse each day.

> There's no life in his eyes and
> his shoulders sag. He's lost
> interest in the things that
> were once so important to
> him. He finds little joy in his
> family now; not even little Elly
> has the charm to pull him
> from the depths. He's short
> with the boys and worse with
> me.

> He says he wants to get
> things done, but then sits in
> front of the TV. At bedtime,
> he complains because his life
> is "out of control" and that he
> is a "no longer happy," re-

frains I hear every day now.
I truly believe that since he's
never experienced adversity in
his own life, he has few skills
for coping. He doesn't seem
to know how to help himself,
and I don't know how to help
him either.

Rereading that letter years later,
I see clearly the signs of Steve's depression, for it reads like a script for an antidepressant advertisement. But I wrote
that in the early 1990s, about five years
after Prozac had been introduced and well
before there was widespread awareness
of the symptoms associated with mental
illnesses. With no medical understanding to describe what I saw, I believed that
Steve's lows were, in the popular vernacu-
lar of the day, a midlife crisis. I was beginning to think that he wanted out of our
marriage.

Chapter 5

Impaired Thinking

Analyzing the progression of Steve's mental health problems—especially how we unwittingly adjusted our lives to incorporate changes in his personality—was challenging. The deterioration of one's mental well-being is easier to understand retrospectively and with an enhanced knowledge of how the mind works. But in those earlier years, it was like living in a fog, where previous life experiences helped little in understanding or dealing with the emerging crisis. Through the first several years of Steve's troubles I had only a slight sense that something was medically wrong. Instead, I viewed what was happening through the context of our relationship. He insisted that he still loved me. His actions sometimes suggested otherwise.

As Steve struggled through this period of his life, when he was trying to make a go of Plasquip, he moved in and out of depression, unable to engage wholly in work or family life. But he didn't fully abandon these things either. There were many times when everything felt normal, when he had a good day in the office and we had an enjoyable family meal together. Afterwards, he might linger at the kitchen table talking or head to the garage with the boys. But low moods eventually overtook the good ones, and six months after the Halloween party, he agreed to see a psychiatrist. I went with him to his first appointment, as well as to most of his monthly visits, for there was still an understanding between us that we would face what was happening together. After talking alone with Steve, the psychiatrist met with the two of us, serving as a kind of marriage counselor as we struggled to reconcile our differences over an increasing number of issues: family finances, his lack of effort at Plasquip, the unfair division of labor in our home, and Steve's distancing himself from family and friends. After several visits, the psychiatrist diagnosed him with situational depression, a temporary mental health condition that occurs during particularly stressful times in people's life. The financial setback from selling the Ohio farm weighed heavily on both of us, and the series of job changes were difficult for Steve to come back from. He seemed stuck in a downward spiral, and the doctor prescribed Prozac.

I continued to think of Steve's troubles as something that would pass and was mollified by his willingness to see a doctor. That wasn't necessarily a given for an ex-farm boy who, like most people in the 1990s, saw the inability to control one's mood as a weakness. Steve continued to see his Plasquip customers, maybe not every day but several times a week, and outwardly our family looked intact: Together Steve and I attended the kids' school and sports activities, vacationed with the Bokermanns, and joined friends regularly for card club on Saturday evening. Mostly, though, life lumbered forward, for Steve remained an unhappy version of his earlier self.

One of the few things Steve still seemed genuinely interested in was his involvement with SAE's Pittsburgh chapter, which he'd joined shortly after we moved to Pennsylvania. Even after quitting his job at SAE headquarters, he remained active with the local chapter. He attended monthly meetings and served in various leadership positions, just as he had done in Dayton. But there was one significant difference. Instead of championing the engineering society's mission as he once did, he often focused on the problems he saw within the organization. This change in thinking—more so the degree to which it took over his life—was at the base of what would eventually be diagnosed as a psychosis, which would remain with him for the rest of his life.

Steve's psychosis didn't manifest in the more familiar forms depicted in movies, where auditory or visual hallucinations alert the audience that something is seriously wrong. Instead, his psychosis emerged in the guise of skewed perceptions, where what was once important no longer mattered, and, conversely, what was tangentially relevant to his life mushroomed into obsessions. The lens through which Steve saw the world changed. Once gregarious and openly enthusiastic about new people and ideas, he became suspicious and less amenable to other points of view, especially those relating to government or big business. He began championing the little guy or people who stood up to the establishment. And his ability to think logically through issues and make good decisions was also compromised. Understanding these changes would take years, and through the in-between time, I was utterly confused and extremely unhappy. I struggled daily to hold on to what we once had, buoyed by my sister's support and driven by an unquestioned resolve to stay married to a man who often acted like a stranger.

• • •

"What do you mean, they didn't plant a tree for Tim?" I ask Steve, trying to make sense of what he's telling me. (Tim is not his real name.) A year has passed since the Halloween party, and Steve and I are eating at an Italian sub shop near the newspaper office where I work. We try getting together for lunch once a week. It gives us time alone, away from the pressures of home. For an hour the conversation usually flows more harmoniously as we put aside the growing differences between us. But I can see that's not going to happen today. Steve has just come from a meeting with SAE's executive vice president, Jack (not his real name). He'd called Steve earlier in the day to ask about disparaging remarks Steve had made at a recent Pittsburgh chapter meeting. He wanted Steve to come to headquarters to talk about it. By the time he got to the sub shop, Steve was revved from his meeting with Jack.

Jack had become SAE's vice president and general manager the year before Steve started working there. He'd met Jack on several occasions before then, once when Jack visited the Dayton chapter shortly after he had been tapped to head the organization. Jack was also the

one who presented Steve with his Outstanding Young Engineers award. The
previous VP had been with SAE for decades, and Jack's appointment, as expected, brought a number of changes to the
organization. One was the creation of the
SAE Foundation, which supported high
school math and science curricula and
provided scholarships to promising engineering students. Steve had gotten along
well with Jack when he worked at SAE,
but in years since his departure, Steve
had become more disgruntled with the
direction the society was going.

"When Jack called this morning, he
said he wanted to talk to me about what
I'd said at the chapter meeting," Steve
says to me after the waitress takes our
order. "I told him that I would meet with
him as long as he was willing to talk to
me about what happened to the money
SAE collected as a memorial for Tim." An
SAE staff engineer, Tim had passed away
unexpectedly several months before Steve
quit.

"Tim died several years ago," I say.
"Why are you so worried about his memo-

rial now?"

"When they asked us to donate in his memory, they said it was to have a tree planted at headquarters," Steve says. "But they never planted a tree."

"Is that what your meeting with Jack was about?" I ask, still trying to piece together what Steve is talking about.

"Yes. Yes," Steve says. "That and what I said at the chapter meeting. But we never got around to talking about that. I told him I wasn't willing to discuss that until I got an answer about how the money for the tree was spent. When I got there, Jack was in a meeting with some managers. He stood in the doorway of the conference room like he was going to take care of my concern quick and easy. He said that they'd collected about $1,200 and the money had been donated to the SAE Foundation in Tim's memory. Like that was that, and we didn't need to talk about it anymore."

In the years since leaving SAE, Steve became more concerned about the newly created foundation. He didn't object to supporting engineering education, but he was wary of what percentage of the foundation's money was actually targeted for that. According to Steve, SAE never disclosed how foundation funds were spent. He also was concerned that the foundation would distract SAE from its core mission of advancing mobile technology.

Sitting with Steve at lunch four years after Tim passed away, I see he's still deeply agitated.

"It's over," I say. "We've got more important things to worry about."

"But when they asked us to donate, they said it was to plant a tree," he says.

I try changing the subject again, but it doesn't work. Our hour together won't be as I wanted.

He continues: "I said, 'Jack, are you sure? Because when we were asked to give, we were told the money would be for something else.' I chose my words carefully. I didn't want to lead Jack to a particular conclusion about how the money was supposed to be spent. I wanted the records to show or someone at SAE to say that we had been told the money was for planting a tree."

Sensing Steve's unwillingness to back down, Jack moved from the open doorway and invited him into his office. There he told Steve that he'd tried to find out, but the several people at SAE he talked to couldn't remember what was said when the money was collected, so it was given to the foundation in Tim's memory.

"When I heard this, I started yelling. And when I did, he kind of implied that if I didn't settle down I'd be thrown out. But I wasn't going to go easy."

Steve is flushed. I ask him to lower his voice.

"I told him, 'Jack, I came here to get an answer, and if you think you're going to throw out a loyal SAE member without a better answer than that, you're going to have your hands full because I won't go without a fight.' " Steve says. "I wanted someone within SAE to verify what I remembered about the money, so Jack wouldn't think I was making it up."

Jack then offered to phone several people to see if they could remember how the money was to be used, but no one could recall. Then he asked Steve to recommend someone to call. Steve suggested a woman who'd worked in Tim's area and whose mother had passed away around the same time as Tim.

"I thought she might remember what had been said," Steve says. "When Jack asked her about the money, right away she said that some people thought it would be nice to plant a tree at headquarters and have a plaque with Tim's name on it.

"When I heard her answer, I jumped up," Steve says. "I'd heard what I needed to hear, and I was going to leave. I said to Jack, 'There it is. I've heard all I need to hear.' Jack looked puzzled that I was leaving. Before walking out I yelled back at him: 'Jack, you need to start listening to your people!' I was so relieved when I heard her answer. I knew that that had been the plan all along."

Watching Steve tell his story, I wonder how he can focus on something that no longer matters to us. I also wonder how this intelligent man can think that someone's suggestion constitutes "a plan." I'm still several years away from hearing the phrase "thought disorder," a psychiatric diagnosis that includes disorganized and illogical thought processes. And finally, I wonder why I continue to stand by a man who cares so little for his family or for me.

As Steve sips his coffee, I sense how triumphant he feels by what happened in Jack's office. The lunch hour is over; I will return to work while he goes back to whatever he does while our life continues spiraling downward. I'm working two jobs, and yet I had to borrow three thousand dollars from Nancy and Mark to pay this year's real estate taxes. It's a loan that won't be repaid for twenty years, but I don't know that when I accept the money. Despite what is obvious as I look back on our conversation, I still clung to the belief that our lives would one day be normal again. That when Steve was more successful at Plasquip, his focus on the engineering society would fade.

And I don't contradict what he's told me because I know it will only exacerbate the situation. But I do ask, "Why are you so focused on this now? Tim's died years ago, and you're going on about SAE not planting a tree. Why is this so important?"

"Somebody has to stand up for what's right," Steve says with relish, a phrase I hear often as his campaign against SAE accelerates. His fight to have a tree planted will broaden to include other concerns about SAE. It will continue for another four years, until a psychiatrist finally diagnoses Steve with chronic psychosis, a mental condition with symptoms that are alleviated by antipsychotic medication.

• • •

As Steve's mind became less stable, he was often drawn into issues that hadn't concerned him before. In our first two decades together, he showed little interest in social or political matters, but had strong opinions about the effect of technology on people's lives. When Ralph Nader campaigned for automotive safety in the 1960s, Steve thought he'd make an ideal candidate when his name was ban-

died about for the 1972 presidential elec-
tion, the first time Steve and I were eli-
gible to vote. And when the director of the
National Highway Traffic Safety Administration during the Carter Administration
pushed for air bags in cars before Steve
felt they had been properly developed, he
voted against President Carter's re-elec-
tion in 1980.

As the psychosis emerged, though,
his interests and thinking changed significantly. I was unaware of the degree to
which this was happening then. It became clearer only after his mind stabilized
and he shared with me the box of correspondence he kept during his campaign
against SAE. The box was the kind reams
of paper come in, and across the top and
sides he'd scrawled, "SAE, Ax Jack!" In it
he kept the correspondence on a sundry
of issues, each marked with the date and
time it was sent or received. He also filed
contemporaneous notes whenever he met
with someone from SAE. That's where I
found a detailed account of his meeting
with Jack.

Reading through the box of

correspondence, I better understood the degree to which Steve's thinking changed. Although the main complaint against SAE was the tree, his litany of concerns widened. He once wrote SAE about a picture of a car engine that had been improperly displayed in one of its publications. He also took issue with the engineering society because there were fewer technical people on staff. There was correspondence between him and SAE's board of directors in which he raised concerns about "a slight misappropriation of funds" because the money collected for the tree had been donated to the foundation. His letter prompted the board to conduct an independent audit. A copy of the audit report—which found that the "monies collected have been properly accounted for"—was also in the box.

When Steve received his 25-year SAE membership pin, he returned it in protest, which resulted in another flurry of letters between him and several people within the organization. Eventually, Steve wrote a letter to the president of SAE's board of directors to express his concern

as to whether Jack was "the best person
for this important position in our society,"
a question eerily reminiscent of the one
his former boss posed to Steve several
years earlier.

Not everything in the box related to
SAE. After seeing a news segment about
the increasing problem of street gangs
on a Pittsburgh television station, Steve
wrote to the station manager and complained about its superficial coverage of
blacks in Pittsburgh: "These all-white
stations need to be more in touch with the
real issues," he wrote. He added that if re-
porters didn't do a better job of getting to
the root of stories, "gangs will weed YOU
out for wearing the wrong color or driving
the wrong color of car."

Like his effort to have the tree
planted, Steve's newfound awareness of
how street gangs were portrayed on local
television station seemed out of the blue,
until I learned about a man he'd met who
lived in a subsidized housing complex on
Pittsburgh's North Side. Like Steve, the
elderly man drove a Rambler. Steve occasionally visited his home, and I met him

several times when Steve worked on his car at our house. Once the two of them even spent an evening going from bar to bar in Pittsburgh's Hill District, then a run-down neighborhood east of downtown. These were uncommon experiences for Steve, who seemed fascinated by his friend's background and lifestyle. The two visited on and off for about a year, until Steve's full-scale mental breakdown put an end to their atypical alliance. It was yet another oddity in a husband whose thinking and behaviors were increasingly different from what they had been.

Chapter 6

Pushing the Limits

Tucked away in a cardboard box in our basement is a picture Luke drew during a particularly tense period in our home. It was a fifth-grade art project in which he was asked to tell a story through a series of scenes. Using a thick black marker, he divided the picture into four frames. In the first was a stick figure standing upright, his arms raised in delight with a word bubble that reads, "Billy plays." The next frame shows the figure alongside a leafless tree with the words "Billy works." In the third, Luke drew dark, gnarly branches jutting from a blackened tree trunk next to an upright figure with the phrase "Billy runs" across the top. In the final frame, the stick boy is lying under a solid black tree, his arms and legs jutting at odd angles from his round black body. Over the prostrated child are the words "Billy dies."

I re-discovered the picture more than a decade after it was drawn, when putting away less-ominous artifacts from Luke's childhood. It had been slipped into the box amid other childhood memen- tos. Like feathers from the wild turkey he killed with his great-grandfather's 22 single-shot rifle when he was ten. And the scrap of paper on which he noted the ex- act time his last school recess ended: 27 minutes and 14 seconds after 1 o'clock on the afternoon on June 7, 1995. He would be entering middle school next year, and there wouldn't be any more recess.

Finding that drawing reminded me of the overarching concern I had for John, Luke, and Elly growing up amid an unrav- eling home life. As Steve's mission against SAE gained momentum, he was often at odds with the kids, especially the boys. He'd naturally been at his fatherly best in the children's earlier years, when caring for them was less complicated. My forte as a parent was in my steadfast, nurturing nature. Following my mother's example, I wanted them to feel secure in their home life, that they understood what was expected of them and what they could expect from us. I monitored their homework and held fast to routines. But all that was changing. At times our home felt like an emotional minefield, and each of us in our own way was learning to tiptoe through it. Luke's drawing seemed a reflection of the confusion that stemmed from the turmoil in our home. And that upheaval was tied to another emerging concern, that Steve's playful interaction with the children—a hallmark of his parenting style—was increasingly more dangerous.

• • •

"What are you doing with that car?" I yell to Steve from the deck at the back of our house. I'm washing the big picture windows outside our living room. They overlook the pasture and woods behind our home, and I like clean windows in the fall, when I can see the gently rolling hills that lay beyond the far end of our property. Today, however, I see Steve on the Ferguson tractor pulling a broken-down Rambler from behind the barn.

When we moved to Pennsylvania, I often teased Steve about not minding how many old cars he had, as long as he kept them out of sight. I meant tucked away in the barn, but that didn't happen. Instead, he had a half-dozen non-working Ramblers behind the barn, out of sight from the road, yes, but not from our living room windows.

A year has passed since Steve's ominous meeting in Jack's office, and his crusade against SAE has spilled over into our everyday life. Now he does little things to remind us: On one of the many sweatshirts he received for recruiting new members he painted the word SUX beneath the SAE logo. On a refrigerator magnet that bore the organization's logo, he altered the words to read: "Improve SAE, AX JACK." Although menacing, Steve carried out these unwelcomed reminders of his feud with SAE lightheartedly, somehow turning them into a joke between himself and the rest of the family. I mostly ignored this odd manifestation of his crusade, and instead deliberately didn't serve coffee in SAE mugs or neglected to put the offending sweatshirt back in his drawer after washing it.

Although I disliked what he was doing, I also knew I wasn't dealing with a completely rational man. And I felt reassured by his monthly visits to a psychiatrist, for certainly the doctor would know if something was seriously wrong. I kept thinking—hoping, really—that when life evened out, when Plasquip became a sure thing, his focus on the engineering society would pass. And even though his mood was erratic, I wasn't really afraid that he would harm the children or me. More so I worried that he might hurt himself. During one visit to the psychiatrist, I listened in dismay when he told her about wanting to drive his Rambler through the front door of Jack's home.

"Do you know where Jack lives?" the psychiatrist asked.

"No," Steve said. "I know I saw his address once when I worked at SAE."

"Have you tried to get the address?"

she asked.

"I tried but couldn't find it," he said.

Then he added: "I really just want Jack to know how serious I am about trying to improve SAE. I wouldn't want to hurt him, especially his wife, if she were there."

Hearing this, my heart softened, for as irrational as Steve could be, he never wanted to hurt anyone. I knew that he was deeply unhappy and struggled daily with work. Although Prozac had initially improved his mood, he slipped frequently into depression. To help him focus, the psychiatrist recently prescribed an attention deficit medication, the stimulant Ritalin.

This was the mid-1990s, and mental health practitioners were less aware of the impact stimulants might have when someone is taking an antidepressant. Only with time would doctors understand the potential danger inherent in the pharmacological combination. For Steve, adding Ritalin would greatly exacerbate the mania when his mood swung high the following year.

• • •

Seeing Steve through the living room window, I think he's towing the Rambler to the garage, where he'll retrieve a part before putting it back behind the barn. The '65 Rambler he uses daily often needs fixing, so his hauling a nonworking car to the garage isn't unusual. He also knows I don't want a junk car left in front of our home. If it were up to him, he'd arrange all the parts cars conveniently near the garage. But I like things neat, tucked away and out of sight. I'm not a finicky housekeeper, but I hate clutter. With such limited time now, I'm learning to live with the illusion of order, where kitchen counters are cleared in the evening and broken-down cars are parked neatly out of sight.

Instead of heading to the garage, though, Steve drives the Fergie to the deck where I am standing. Scampering up the hill behind him are five excited children—John, Luke, Elly, and two neighborhood kids. When he shuts off the engine, I ask again what he's doing.

"We're going to push the Rambler down the hill," he says, unhooking the car at the steepest point of the backyard hill. His answer is matter of fact, as if doing this is as common as kicking a soccer ball around the yard.

"It doesn't have an engine or transmission," he says reassuringly, as if that makes what he's doing more okay.

"Why?" I ask, puzzled. I don't want to know about the engine or transmission, but why a 44-year-old father would undertake such an activity with his children. Especially with other kids around.

"It'll be fun," he says. "The kids want to do it."

"Yeah," I reply sarcastically. "I'm sure it was their idea."

Steve smiles brightly up to me, something that doesn't happen much anymore.

• • •

Although at times Steve distances himself from the family, there are times

when he seems to enjoy being with us.
There are still moments of tenderness,
like when he reads five-year-old Elly bedtime stories. He also enjoys telling ten-
year-old Luke tales about growing up on a
dairy farm when he tucks him in at night.
Luke still has night terrors and likes
having his father with him when falling
asleep. A half-hour after Luke goes to bed,
I often find Steve sitting on the floor next
to him, both of them sound asleep. Steve's
head rests on the mattress, and Luke is
touching his father's hair. Steve always
liked having someone rub his head; if he's
stressed or restless at night, it helps him
fall asleep. The morning after Steve's bicycle accident, when he was knocked unconscious, the only thing he could recall
from the previous twenty hours was Luke
standing by his hospital bed touching his
hair.

    Despite his growing separation
from us, Steve still drives John to ice
hockey practice, sometimes standing with
the other fathers at the edge of the rink
watching their sons skate. When he's low,
though, he sits alone in his Rambler or

drives around until practice is over. Odd-
ly, for the past several months, Steve has
taken to spending more time in his car,
either driving aimlessly on the back roads
around our area or, when parked in our
driveway, lying in the back seat. I'll find
him there, his six-foot frame curled up,
his head resting on a small pillow. When I
ask what's wrong, he might say he's angry
at something I said or, more likely, that he
doesn't want to be around anyone. Sometimes he'll stay there for an hour or two,
and I'll busy myself in the house, listening
for the front door to open and him to slip
back into our life.

• • •

Standing below the back deck,
Steve looks excitedly up at me, happier
than I've seen him in a long time. I don't
like what he's doing, especially with other
children around. But it's better than lying alone in the back seat of a Rambler.
When I turn to leave, Steve calls up to me,
"Don't worry," he says. "We'll be safe."
Steve has always been more

physically daring than I, even before the
onset of his mental health problems. But
he's also keenly aware of the dangers
inherent in whatever he's doing, whether
racing his Porsche in an autocross or
properly securing jack stands before
sliding beneath a car. Growing up on a
dairy farm and trained as an engineer, he
knows how things can fail. He frequently
invokes Murphy's Law, that if something
can go wrong, it will. He was especially
careful when working with the boys,
warning them about keeping their pant
legs clear of the power takeoff shaft when
driving the Fergie. Or to be watchful of
animals darting onto the trail when they
ride their dirt bikes. In our years together,
I don't think I've ever stood next to a
railing without Steve grabbing it first to
make sure it was safe. As I watch him
interacting with the children, I wonder if
that's changed too. Can I still trust that
pushing the Rambler down the hill is
safe? I want to, but I'm no longer sure.
When Steve turns towards the children,
who have reached the top of the hill
behind our house, I don't go back to

washing windows, preferring instead to work inside, away from Steve's backyard shenanigans. I do that more too, look the other way when I don't like what I see.

Later Steve tells me what happened. On the first run down, everything went as expected. The kids pushed the car while Steve ran alongside, steering it around the trees. As it neared the bottom of the yard, he steered into a small tree at the edge of the pasture. It thudded to a stop. The kids surveyed the crushed bumper and hood before Steve towed it back up the hill for a second run. The next time Steve intentionally turned the car into a stump, causing the right front end to raise dangerously high and the stump to go under the car. "I thought the car might flip," Steve said.

Despite the children's pleas, he nixed a third run down the hill, suggesting instead that they push the Rambler through the pasture and into the small pond at the far end of our property. It would be safer because the hill wasn't as steep: "We wouldn't get up as much speed going through the pasture," he explained.

Like before, Steve ran alongside the car as it bumped across the uneven ground. The kids pushed, sometimes running to keep up with the car and other times using their combined strength to keep it moving. When the front wheels crested the bank of the pond, the car splashed into the water and the children whooped with delight. Slowly the Rambler settled to the muddy bottom, with only the hood and trunk lid visible above the surface of the water.

Then they turned their attention to getting the car out of the water. Laying a 2x10 from the shore to the trunk, Steve and John made their way to the car's roof, where they threaded a log chain through the two vent windows. Hooking the chain to the Fergie, they pulled the Rambler from the pond, the tractor straining against the weight of the waterlogged vehicle. As they pulled it back up the hill, the tires flung mud everywhere. I wasn't happy about Steve's odd Saturday afternoon adventure, but I held my thoughts in pursuit of family harmony. Later that night I called Nancy.

"It just doesn't seem right," I said. "I wonder what the neighbor girls' parents thought when they told them what happened at our house this afternoon?"

"At least no one got hurt," Nancy said. "Be thankful for that."

"But if he keeps this up, someone might," I said. "Remember what he did with the gunpowder." Earlier in the summer, Steve wanted to get rid of some old shotgun shells that may no longer be safe to use. He and the boys emptied the shell cartridges and snaked a trail of gunpowder up the driveway, then lit a match and watched it burn. It turned out to be less pyrotechnic than they had hoped, but Nancy and I agreed it was still an odd thing for a father to do with his children.

We both knew that what Steve did with the kids wasn't normal, but I explained it away as a more extreme version of the kinds of things he'd been doing for years. Once, when Elly was four and we talked about how animals burrowed in the leaves to keep warm at night, Steve suggested they try it. That night they wrapped themselves in sweatpants and hooded sweatshirts to keep the leaves from their face, "like an animal's skin," Steve said, and snuggled beneath a blanket of leaves. They stayed out half the night, until temperatures dipped into the 40s and drove them inside.

Eventually I associated Steve's pushing the Rambler into the pond with what was being reported in the news at that time. Several weeks earlier a woman from South Carolina made national news when she drove her Mazda Protégé into a lake, killing her two young sons. It was a sensational story, and TV viewers watched in horror as the sodden car was pulled from the lake. As Steve's fragile mind teetered between reality and insanity, was he influenced by the strange and fateful action of a woman several hundred miles away? Possibly, for as I gained a better understanding of how mental imbalance leads to odd fixations, I saw other examples of Steve's fascination with the macabre when his mind was unstable.

After one psychotic break, Steve became captivated with the death of a local man from a botched castration by his transsexual wife. It was sensational news for our area, and the media covered it from her arrest to the trial and beyond. Steve followed the investigation obsessively, to the point that I asked him not to talk to me about it anymore. I became aware of the extent of his fixation when I discovered a folder of newspaper articles that he'd clipped about the case, from the man's death until six years later, when the woman was accused of writing threatening letters from her jail cell.

Steve's obsessions weren't always macabre. A common symptom of mental instability is impulsive and over-the-top spending. Steve is naturally frugal, so his spending sprees usually involved cheap and oftentimes unnecessary household items on sale. Once he came home with more than $200 in merchandise from the Dollar Store. Another time it was several cartloads of soda from the grocery store. There was a period when he excessively bought Alberto VO5 shampoo because it was cheap, only a dollar for a 12.5-ounce bottle. "They'll never go bad," he'd say

when he came home with several more
bottles of shampoo. Once, when stashing
them away beneath our bathroom sink, I
decided to try something. Steve responds
more to visual arguments than verbal
ones, so I snaked nearly thirty bottles of
the multi-colored shampoo across the
bathroom floor and into our bedroom,
creating a visual that finally put an end to
his buying shampoo.

• • •

In the year leading up to Steve' first
full-blown psychotic break, I was deeply
confused by all that was happening. I
knew something was seriously wrong,
but I didn't see the changes as a medical
problem. I still loved him and wanted our
marriage to last, but I also had to think
about the children. Was my staying with
Steve and allowing him to interact as he
did endangering them? What if the car
had flipped? Or the snaking gunpowder
had burned someone? He'd always been
a good father and husband. Was that
changing too? After one very bitter argu-

ment about his unrelenting effort against
SAE—there had been many—I accused
him of not being there for his children.

"They need you now, not after you
fix SAE," I said, pushing hard for him to
acknowledge his responsibilities.

"I have more important things to do
now," he answered. "As far as I'm concerned, the government can take care of
them."

The words cut to my core, loop-
ing obsessively in my mind. How could I
stay with someone who'd strayed so far
from who he once was. I didn't tell Nancy
what Steve said for a very long time, too
ashamed to be with someone who said
such things. But I did stay. Ending our
marriage would mean I had failed. And
being on my own with three children felt
overwhelming. For me, Steve's words
became emblematic of the gulf between
us. A reminder of how far apart we had
grown. He was no longer the man I married, nor the loving father he'd once been.

Despite the issues that divided us,
I stayed, in part because he could still be
loving towards me. I still went with him

every month to the psychiatrist, and I saw
how he struggled to balance work and
family with his deeply held convictions
about SAE. And he told me often how he
appreciated my staying with him as he
worked through these issues. Occasionally he wrote me notes. In one, written a
month before he would leave the family to
pursue without interference his campaign
against SAE, he thanked me for caring so
much for our family. In another, he wrote:
"If I can get this (SAE) out of my system,
I think I'll be able to go on again and be
the man I was. Please believe this, and
don't blame yourself. You're perfect, and I
wouldn't change a thing about you."

Steve and I occasionally wrote notes
to each other in the years leading up to
his breakdown, especially after we argued.
Steve wasn't naturally inclined to express
himself in writing, but he did so more
frequently then. Writing allowed us to
communicate without the emotional intensity that often occurred when we were
together. Our written words were gen-
tler and sweeter than our spoken ones. I
especially treasured the whimsical notes,

those reflecting the humorous, upbeat man I'd fallen in love with. Following one fight, he wrote on the outside of a business envelope: "Linda—Loving Wife: This letter describes what I am in one word." Inside was the word "rambler," which he'd cut from a dictionary. He taped the word to a piece of paper and on it wrote, "Please keep one Rambler in your life; I'll love you forever." After he was diagnosed with bipolar disorder and was taking the mood stabilizer lithium, he gave me a step stool that he bought at a garage sale. In a note accompanying the gift he wrote, "The steps swing up and down, like me. To prevent problems, I put some lithium grease on them." The one I treasure most was a Christmas tree ornament he made the year of his breakdown. With a tiny bolt he fastened two Popsicle sticks to form a cross. On it he wrote, "Linda, Keep me as your cross a little longer." These tender exchanges were the tether that kept me by his side.

Several months after pushing the Rambler into the pond, though, there would be an accident, one involving another of Steve's questionable undertakings with the kids. It set off a series of events that led to Steve and me living apart.

Chapter 7

The Accident

"I want to show you something," Luke says when I pull into the driveway. It's late afternoon on a Sunday in December, a month after Steve and the kids pushed the Rambler into the pond. Elly and I are coming back from a children's concert in Pittsburgh, part of a series of shows supported by local art organizations that introduces kids to theater, dance, and music. We've had season tickets to the children's program since moving to the Pittsburgh area. At first only the boys and I went, until Elly was old enough to join us. Then all five attended for a while, until ice hockey and other activities pulled John and Luke away. Now Steve stays home with them while Elly and I go.

Luke, who recently turned eleven, is

home alone when we get there. Steve and
John left an hour ago for a high school ice
hockey game. The plan is for me to stop at
home and get Luke for an after-theater ice
cream treat. When we arrive, he's waiting
on the front stoop, but I see immediately
that he isn't ready. First he wants to show
us a new target Steve made for his BB
gun. I hesitate to get out of the car. Sunday evenings are when I get ready for the
workweek, and I was hoping to make this
a quick turnaround. But Luke is determined to show us the target, and he motions us through the kitchen and into the
side yard. Reluctantly, I get out of the car,
and Elly follows me. Stepping through the
kitchen door, I see Luke's BB gun leaning against the back of the garage. He's
not allowed to use it without an adult
around. Luke has especially keen eyesight
for distance, and Steve occasionally comes
up with new targets for him to practice
his aim. This one is made from the brass
end of a 12-gauge shotgun shell, the gunpowder and BBs removed. A small round
piece of metal about the size of a candy
Kiss sits on a tree stump thirty feet from

where we stand. Embedded in the metal is a primer cap the size of a kernel of corn. It has a tiny bit of gunpowder in it that will explode if struck.

Luke has always liked the outdoors, while John prefers sitting inside for hours building Lego cars and trucks. When Luke was younger, he pretended to hunt in the woods behind our home. Wearing the coonskin cap and cowboy vest we bought him for Christmas, he'd head to the woods. Other times I'd see him standing quietly in the backyard watching a deer at a salt block mounted on a sawed-off fence post in the pasture. He'd catch the deer's gaze and slowly move toward it, seeing how close he could get before it bolted to the woods.

Seeing the new target, I ask Luke whether it's safe. I don't expect anything other than yes for an answer, but I ask anyway. I always do. I've never been comfortable with the kids' dirt bikes and BB guns. But seeing Luke's natural interest in the outdoors, I reluctantly supported Steve when he encouraged these activities.

Besides Luke's BB gun, there are two other guns in our house, a 20-gauge shotgun and a 22 bolt-action rifle, both hand-me-downs from Steve's parents. His family used them to hunt small game and occasionally shoot varmints on their farm. Although I didn't grow up around guns, I was happy to have the rifle when I came across a raccoon clinging to the sliding door handle on our back deck when we first moved to Pennsylvania. Steve shot it with the 22, concerned that its unusual behavior might mean it was rabid. Steve hunted with his dad when he was growing up, and Luke can't wait until he turns twelve and gets a junior license. We live in a school district that closes on the first day of buck season, and hunting is a way of life around here. So when Steve wanted to get Luke the Daisy Sharpshooter for Christmas last year, I agreed.

Seeing the new target in the distance, I check to see where Elly is. She's behind me, sitting on the cement steps leading to the kitchen. Elly has the easy-going manner of a youngest child, learning early that nap or playtime may be

disrupted by her older brothers' activities. She has a remarkable ability to con-
tent herself wherever she is, even as we
wait for Luke to show us the target. He's
standing about three feet in front of me,
the BB gun aimed at the tiny brass cap on
the tree stump. Shrugging his shoulders
to settle the gun into place, he pulls the
trigger.

I hear the sounds simultaneously.
The gun firing and Luke's awful shriek.
His head jerks backwards, and his hands
fly to his right eye. His legs buckle, and
he slumps to the ground. When I bend to
him, I see blood trickling from between
his cupped fingers.

• • •

Luke underwent surgery the next
morning to suture the wounded eye. The
kernel-sized primer cap entered through
the pupil at the lower right edge of his
gray-blue iris. It didn't pass through the
eye, which meant the doctors would probably be able to save the eyeball. The cap
lodged at the back of the eye, partially

detaching the retina and bouncing off the optic nerve. The eye was too bloody for the doctors to retrieve the metal piece or determine the extent of the damage. After the blood drained, they would perform a second surgery to remove the primer cap and reattach the retina. Luke was given antibiotics. If the eye got infected, there was a small chance the infection could spread to his good eye, the doctor said. Luke had to stay in bed for the ten days between surgeries because jostling may cause the cap to move.

The commotion of Luke's accident refocused Steve's attention from SAE to family. Together we cared for him, moving his bed into the living room so someone was always nearby. We played games or watched TV on the new set Grandma and Grandpa Schmitmeyer brought with them when they traveled from Ohio to help out. Knowing how much Luke liked the outdoors, Steve found a fish tank in the classified ads of the newspaper and set it next to his bed. And at night he told Luke bedtime stories. I felt reassured watching Steve care for Luke, for it helped alleviate the nagging yet unspoken thoughts I had about the target Steve made.

For several weeks following the second surgery, the doctor shone a light into the injured eye. Sometimes Luke imagined seeing a pinprick of light, and we became hopeful. But as the weeks passed, it became clear that scar tissue on the optic nerve meant Luke no longer had vision in that eye. The prolonged uncertainty was difficult for Luke, who grew sullen and angry, especially with me, a safe target for his fears and frustrations.

Even little Elly sensed Luke's low mood. About an hour after she went to bed several weeks after the accident, I found her in the kitchen fumbling through a shoebox full of Crayons.

"What are you doing, honey?" I asked.

"I want to make Luke a pretty picture," she said.

"But you've already made him lots of pretty pictures," I said, reminding her of the array of artwork decorating the living room wall by Luke's bed. "You need to be in bed," I said firmly. "You can draw a picture tomorrow."

"I want to do it now," came Elly's uncharacteristically insistent response.

Surprising even myself, I relented. I'm fairly strict about bedtime schedules, but I also knew that Elly would sleep better if she drew Luke a picture. When she finished, she taped it alongside the others and said, "Now he'll be happy when he wakes up."

With the commotion surrounding Luke's accident, I thought very little about how it happened. Whenever I did, I couldn't shake the feeling that Steve may not have acted responsibly. Was the target that he set up inherently dangerous? I knew Luke shot at the brass end of a shotgun shell, but I didn't know that shotgun shells had primer caps. Nor that they held bits of gunpowder. Initially I thought a piece of the brass shell had broken off and struck Luke's eye. With time I learned differently.

Even though I didn't understand the target, I did know that Steve was more daring in his interactions with the children. And that I had done nothing to stop him. If I'd stood up to him, would Luke still see with both eyes?

Several days after Luke's accident, a neighbor stopped by to drop off a pot of chicken soup his wife made. There had been an outpouring of kindness from neighbors and friends when Luke got hurt—get-well cards and phone calls, visits from Luke's fifth-grade classmates, and a steady stream of meals. After thanking my neighbor for the soup, we stood on the cement pad outside our home talking. He was an avid hunter and knew how shotgun shells were made. I could see that he was curious about what happened, so I told him that Luke shot his BB gun at the brass end of a denuded shotgun shell and a piece of metal struck his eye. When I finished, my neighbor turned sharply in an attempt to hide his reaction. But he wasn't quick enough, for I saw a look cross his face that reaffirmed my suspicion. Steve shouldn't have done what he did.

I didn't tell Steve about the conversation, only Nancy, who steered me from worrying about it at the time. "You have to put it behind you," she said. "Luke needs you. Focus on taking care of him."

I know the odds of an exploding primer cap following the same trajectory it did on that cool December afternoon are high, a million to one, I told myself often. Even knowing this, I'll never forget the look on our neighbor's face.

It would be many years before Steve and I talked about the details of Luke's accident. The first in-depth conversation occurred when I was writing about it and asked him to clarify some facts. I did this frequently throughout writing this, asking Steve to share what he remembered as a way of reinforcing my own recollection. He was always willing to do so.

"People need to know," he'd say simply when people asked him how he felt about having such personal and painful details of his life shared with others. To further support my writing, he turned over his own writings from that time: the file of correspondence he'd kept about SAE, notes he'd made before or after appointments with his psychiatrists and therapists, even sketches he'd made about his illness. I'd come into the home office, which I commandeered for writing this, and find a notebook or stack of papers that he'd left for me, with a Stickie note that read, "For your book?"

But we never talked about Luke's accident. The first time I asked about it he was passing the office door. I wanted him to help me recall some of the details, but he seemed reluctant to be drawn into the conversation. Instead of entering the room and sitting on the couch as he usually did, he stood in the hallway, his face half-hidden by the door. He answered my questions but was obviously uncomfortable talking about it. Seeing his distress, I reminded him, "You know it wasn't your fault. You weren't making good decisions then." These are words I use frequently to remind both of us of the ambiguous and imprecise nature of severe mental illnesses. Neither Steve nor I knew at the time of Luke's accident how judgment is affected by a person's mental well-being.

Although Luke never regained sight in his eye, six weeks after the accident he was back in school. By spring the following year, he was playing ice hockey again with his middle school team. He also learned to shoot his BB gun using his left eye, and when he turned twelve a year later, got his junior hunting license.

Nancy and Mark and their family visited over the New Year's holiday. So did our friend Patrick Clune and his family, who travelled from Indiana to be with us. Steve and Patrick had been friends since childhood, and the two of them talked frequently by phone, especially following the series of job changes after leaving SAE. Being with the Clunes and Bokermanns restored a sense of normalcy to our lives. Our families vacationed together often through the years, and seeing Luke play hide and seek with the children—seemingly unaware of the black patch over his right eye—made me hopeful. Steve hadn't talked much about SAE since the accident. Could it have snapped him back to his old self? I was beginning to hope so.

On the last day of their visit, the Bokermanns left early in the morning for their trip back to Illinois, and Patrick and Steve went out for breakfast. Patrick was an accountant for a company that made medical devices, and he could be more objective than me about Steve's prospect for success with Plasquip. Breakfast would be a good chance for them to catch up, away from the commotion of the children. When they returned two hours later, though, Patrick looked worried. He caught my eye and motioned me into the kitchen.

"Where'd you go?" I asked.

"Someplace in town," he said. "I don't know. Howard's I think," dismissing my small talk with a wave of his hand. Leaning confidentially toward me, he whispered, "Is Steve okay?"

His question hit like a brick.

"He's been okay since Luke's accident," I said. "What happened?"

"When did he get so wrapped up with SAE?" Patrick asked. "He couldn't talk about anything else."

Patrick had been aware of Steve's effort to have a tree planted on behalf of the deceased coworker, but not of his wanting to have Jack removed as the executive vice president.

"That's all he talked about," Patrick

said. "I'd deliberately change the subject, but every time I did he'd go right back to SAE." My heart sank. SAE was back in our life, and from what Patrick was telling me, ramped up and unrelenting.

It had been an incredibly difficult year. I couldn't imagine how things could get worse. But they did. A month after the accident, Steve and I would agree to live separately. Two months after that, he had a breakdown.

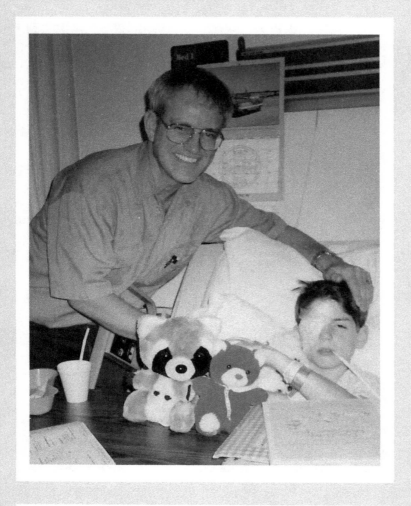

Chapter 8

No Song to Sing

"I don't know what to do," I cry. "This time was different. He was completely out of control."

It's two o'clock in the morning on the first Saturday of the new year, and I'm at the newspaper office. I came here following a harrowing car ride home from a play in Pittsburgh. Steve and I went there to celebrate my birthday. I'm talking to Patrick on the phone in my boss' office. The newsroom opens to a bay of windows, and I am afraid that if I use my desk phone, a passerby might see a light and call the police. I shut the boss' door, but still worry that light might seep around the edges. And to minimize the chance of my boss seeing a lengthy middle-of-the-night phone call to the state of Indiana,

I ask Patrick to call me back. When he does, I sigh, settle deeply into the editor's black armchair, and cry. "Everything has changed," I tell Patrick. "I can't be in the house with him anymore."

When Patrick asks about the children, I answer quickly, pushing down gnawing thoughts about leaving them at home. "He would never hurt the kids," I say. Steve has never physically threatened the children or me, but after last night I'm not sure of anything anymore.

The evening began with a play at Public Theater in Pittsburgh. It was the first time we were alone together since Luke's accident. The play, "Lady Day at Emerson's Bar and Grill," was a re-creation of one of Billie Holiday's last performances. The director had staged it so that the audience sat at café tables, intimating that we were patrons at Emerson's, the Philadelphia nightclub where the jazz singer performed shortly before she died in 1959. The woman playing Holiday sang sensuously and sorrowfully; between songs she shared details of the singer's life. I was touched by the hopelessness that plagued Holiday, a sentiment hauntingly familiar to me now.

Following the performance, we joined friends for a drink at a bar in a once-bustling mill town four miles up the Allegheny River. By midnight, Steve and I were headed home; he was behind the wheel. It usually takes thirty-five minute to get home from the bar, but last night it took more than two hours. Several minutes into the trip, Steve and I began fighting about what we always fight about, his lack of effort at Plasquip and my unwillingness to be with a man who cares so little for his family. This time, though, he went berserk.

• • •

"Do you want me to leave?" Steve yells. "Are you telling me to get out?"

"I only said we can't go on like this. That something has to change."

"If you want me out of your life, I'll leave," he says, his knuckles white against the wheel.

It's late, and there are few cars on

the road. Most are traveling fast. Steve
is too. I beg him to pull over and let me
drive; eventually he turns into a deserted
parking lot, and I take over the wheel.
Again our fight escalates. Now his hand is
on the door latch, and he's threatening to
jump from the car.

"If you want me out, I'll get out.
Right now," he screams. "Tell me! Just tell
me and I'll get out!"

I don't say anything. Over and over
I hear him yell, "Tell me. Tell me now and
I'll leave! Say it. Just say it and I'll jump."

His voice is shrill, unrelenting. I
am crying. Headlights from the oncom-
ing cars dance in my tears. Fanciful.
Surreal. Mesmerized by the brightness, I
move away from his anger to a quiet place
where there is no noise, no pain. There I
see the unfolding drama of our life: The
car snakes through a series of curves the
locals call Mae West Bend. A soft swell
to the right. Now to the left. There I am,
trancelike behind the wheel, swaying
through the voluptuous curves of vaude-
ville's great sex symbol. Steve is there,
too, his hand on the door latch, his angry

face staring down at me. The door is open. His foot dangles near the rushing road-way. His mouth moves mechanically, like a robot propelled by endless energy. There is no sound. Only the motion of his mouth moving in a motorized jaw. And the road-way rushing by.

As I watch this tableau, this unfold-ing moment of our life, time slows. Sec-onds become minutes, minutes feel like hours. My chest heaves. Silent sobs shake me. There is no pain, though. Only letting go. A moving away. We will be safe in this quiet space that sound does not reach. Where no one screams or jumps from the car.

I see us—two hopeless souls cling-ing to our imagined storyline. Our fai-rytale lives. Like the actress who shared Holiday's story. The singer's difficult childhood and long battle with drugs. And years later, her own mother's rejec-tion when she needed her most. Telling us this, the actress sang, "God Bless the Child," lyrics Holiday wrote following that long ago fight with her mother. Steve has turned his back on me too. And on our family. Yet I have no song to sing, only anguished sobs that blend with Steve's unrelenting anger: "If you want me out of your life, tell me! I will jump! I will jump! Tell me and I will jump!"

Will our story end if I say something? Will Steve's leaping to the roadway be our final act? I have no more control over what's happening than Holiday did when her life fell apart. I'm at the end. Giving up. Letting go. My head droops, shutting out the light in my glistening tears. My foot relaxes against the gas pedal; my hands slip from the wheel. Time crawls. The car slows. It is over.

Through the blur I sense Steve's hand in front of me. Big and strong, a farmer's hand. It lightly touches the steering wheel. Little movements. Back and forth. He's guiding us through a curve to the safety of the straightaway. My foot stiffens against the pedal and the car moves slowly forward. United in purpose—his hand on the wheel, my foot on the gas—we steer into another parking lot. Is this how you stop insanity? Is this how you make madness go away?

An entry from my journal written shortly after that car ride reads, "If I become so debilitated and cannot function, he may emerge from his own madness. He did so when Luke had his eye accident. Maybe he'll do so again. For me."

• • •

Thoroughly chilled after talking for hours to Patrick, I hang up. I'm drained and exhausted. I wrap myself in the sleeping bag I brought with me. When I awake an hour later, I see soft morning light seeping around the closed door. The insanity of the night has faded, and I think of the children. If I'm not at home when they get up, they'll worry. I am recharged by the new day, and by my well-worn conviction—that if I can maintain a family routine, if I can hold on to the memory of happier times, one day it will be so. Girded by the light of a new day, I drive home. When the children get up, I'm in the kitchen fixing breakfast.

Later that morning, Steve and I meet with the psychiatrist for a regularly scheduled appointment. As we drive south on the same road we traveled twelve hours earlier, we talk of small things, of the children's weekend schedule, of how we were moved by Billie Holiday's story, and of the awfulness of the car ride home. I tell him of my night at the newspaper office and my long conversation with Patrick. He expresses concern for me and for all that he's put me through. And he says he's sorry. I hesitantly accept his apology. These escalating altercations occur more frequently, but our easy banter no longer lulls me into believing they won't happen again. Last night's fight was beyond anything that has happened before. Scarier. As we make our way to the doctor's office, I am unaware of a change taking place in me, that I am about to tell the psychiatrist that I can no longer live with a man who puts his family second.

As usual, the psychiatrist meets first with Steve, and then I join them. When she asks how things are going, I surprise myself with my answer. "I'm no longer willing to continue like this," I say. It's tentatively presented, but I know if

Steve persists in his crusade against SAE,
I can no longer live in the same house
with him. Hearing my own words, I know
they are true. I just can't do this anymore.

Chapter 9

Living Apart

"Who will read me bedtime stories?" cries Elly when I tell the children that Steve and I are going to live apart. It's the day after our visit to the psychiatrist, my forty-fifth birthday. We are in the living room. Steve and I face one another, he in his Grandma Schmitmeyer's mahogany wood rocker and I at one end of a faded gray couch. Both are hand-me-downs from Steve's parents. When they sold the dairy farm and moved to town the year we married, we inherited some of their furniture. While I love the antique rocker, I hate the sofa, with its scratchy nylon cover and low, sleek look. Elly is in the winged-back chair we bought when renovating our first farmhouse. John and Luke sit on separate sections of the wrap-around couch.

We've had family meetings before, but not often. I like them because they have gravitas, a way of telling the children that what we are going to talk about is important. Five-year-old Elly likes the idea of us coming together to discuss something; John, fifteen, and Luke, eleven, are less enthused, which is obvious in the way they slouch against the back of the couch, their heels dug into the worn red carpet, their arms folded across their chests. Except for the four-and-a-half years that separate them, they could be twins, with their black-brown hair and big dark eyes set in clear, youthful faces. Elly is the fairest of the three, lightly complected with wispy blond hair. She looks more like a Schmitmeyer than the boys, who favor the Kerber family.

Steve and I agreed beforehand that I would tell the children of our decision. We even talked about what I should say: that our separation would be temporary and that their father would live with us again after he finishes what he needs to do with SAE. Drawing in my breath, I begin.

"Your father and I have decided we are going to live apart for a while," I say, scanning the children's faces for their reactions. Hearing John's sharp intake of breath, I quickly add, "In several months, we both hope to live together again."

Luke's response is more controlled. He sits stock-still and says nothing, the eye patch exacerbating his sullenness. When my words register with Elly, she blurts her concern about who will read her bedtime stories. Quickly she slips from the chair and darts from the room, sidestepping John, who reaches out to stop her. She heads down the hallway to her bedroom; John follows.

Glancing at Steve, I see the ache of Elly's outburst in his watery blue eyes. Having to tell the children is especially difficult for him, I know, for even though he's happy to focus solely on SAE for two months, he loves his children. I know this in my heart, despite what he's said about letting the government take care of them. He truly believes our separation is temporary and that when he settles the issue that divides us, he will return to the family fold. I want to believe this but don't think he'll ever be able to let go of his fight until Jack is removed from office. And that's not going to happen. I've told him I think his crusade is personal, that it's connected to his abrupt departure from SAE, but he says that has nothing to do with it. He truly believes that what he's doing is best. He knows that there will be no more SAE when he returns home, though. That's the one condition I've set for our being together again.

To me, telling the children feels like the beginning of the end, for I'm firm in my resolve to live separately if he continues to pursue his mission. Something changed on that harrowing car ride home. A fear I can't ignore. That night at the newspaper office I was startled awake by a reoccurring nightmare, one that intensifies with each iteration. I'm trapped in a room, alone, surrounded by a dozen doors. They're circling me as I search for a way out. I must get away but don't know how. And there are no clues. What is behind each door? Paralyzed by the unknown, I cry out, desperate for an answer.

And like before, my cries wake me. Is that
when I knew I couldn't do this anymore?

No one says a word while John
and Elly are out of the room. I hear the
tick tick tick of the battery-powered clock
hanging on the wall. It's shaped like a
tractor and painted green and yellow, like
a John Deere, the kind of tractors Steve's
father had on his farm. When John and
Elly return, she's tucked into the hollow
of his lean body, his long arms encircling
her. They sit together on the couch, and
I hear him whisper, "I'll read you bedtime
stories until Pop comes back."

John has always been a serious,
responsible child, with a maturity that
belies his age. While Luke vocalizes the
inequities he feels at being asked to do
more around the house, John rarely complains. I'm away most of the day, and before going to work in the morning, I leave
a list of chores for each of the children
on the kitchen counter—burn the trash,
water the chickens and get eggs, run the
sweeper, set the table for supper, clean
the fish tank, mow the grass, whatever is
necessary to keep a household running

when I'm not there. John does his list but also takes it upon himself to make sure Luke and Elly do theirs. "He makes parenting look easy," Nancy used to say when John was a baby. He still does, I think, as I watch him soothe his little sister's concerns.

I motion Elly to me, and she slips through John's arms and sits on my lap. I begin again to explain the new arrangement. Pop is going to live elsewhere but will work from the home office during the day. He will be there when they get off the school bus but will leave before I get home. On weekends, either he or I will be in the house. In two months, on March 15—the day he's agreed to end his efforts at SAE—our family will be together again.

Two days earlier, as Steve and I sat in the psychiatrist's office hashing out the details of our separation, I referred to the date of our reconciliation as the Ides of March, the day the once-loyal Brutus slayed his leader. I think of Steve's efforts that way.

His plan for bringing his campaign to a close was to travel to Detroit for

SAE's annual conference in early March and meet individually with members of the board of directors. Even though none of them had agreed to talk with him, he was certain of his eventual success. When the convention was over, he would have a week to tie up loose ends back in Pennsylvania, and—by the Ides of March, as Steve whimsically and repeatedly referred to the day he would return to the family—his crusade would be over. With a determination fueled by an ascending mania, he never imagined anything but triumph. And I, in my satirical mocking of what he was trying to do, likened his effort to Caesar's downfall. For Steve it was a rallying call, and he talked frequently—and flippantly—of Jack's day of reckoning.

"But where will you live?" Elly asks, breaking free from me and running to her father.

"I get to live in the Scotty," Steve says, wriggling his hands in the air in a familiar gesture of excitement. He knows Elly loves camping in our Scotty trailer, and it's his way of reassuring her that he will be okay.

Following our visit to the psychiatrist, I called a number of local hotels about the cost of long-term stays, but everything was more than we could afford. Steve came up with the idea of living in the camper, a 1962 travel trailer we bought and fixed up shortly after moving to Pennsylvania. It's 16 feet from tongue to bumper and only seven feet wide. When the family camps, Steve has to sleep diagonally across a bed. The only place he can stand upright is in the three-by-three-foot well at the center. A friend who owns land not far from us has agreed to let Steve park it on his property. It has a barn with electricity to run a small ceramic heater. The Scotty also has a small ice box, sink, and stove.

"I'll bring water from home in the five-gallon jug," he tells the children, his voice cheerier than the occasion warrants. "I'm also going to get a little microwave so you can visit and have dinner with me."

"But it's so cold outside," Elly continues with her concerns.

"It is," Steve agrees, for temperatures frequently dip into the single digits in western Pennsylvania in January and February. "I'll have a sleeping bag and grandma's wool quilt. That should keep me warm," he says, placing his big hand above Elly's knee, jiggling it in a familiar gesture of endearment. "I'll be okay," he promises.

My throat tightens and I look away. I hate what is happening, for I feel that nothing good will come of this. He says he will give up his effort by March 15, but his fervor won't let him. And then what?

Over the next several days, we ready the camper for an extended winter stay. Elly, finally okay with what is happening, helps sweep and wash the floor. Steve stocks it with supplies, and I gather towels and bedding. It snows heavily the night before he leaves, complicating his departure.

Getting the camper to the top of our steep driveway involves hooking the Fergie to my car, a station wagon, which in turn is hitched to the camper. John drives the Fergie, and Steve is in the station wagon. Standing at Luke's bedroom window, I watch the train of vehicles spin their way to the top. They make it on the first try. A few minutes later, Luke gets off the school bus and hops into the station wagon. He will help Steve set up the trailer before dark. Two hours later, I hear the Pontiac pull into the driveway and Steve leave in his Rambler. It has finally happened; Steve is gone.

• • •

Steve was happy with our new arrangement. For two months, he could focus solely on what was most important to him while I worked and managed our home life. In a diary he kept sporadically while in the Scotty, he wrote of his first night: "To bed around 9, up at 4:30. Slept in sleeping bag, big quilt, and hooded sweatshirt tied around the neck. Too restrictive. Will sleep in insulated coveralls instead of sleeping bag tonight. Hung clock while making coffee on propane burner to help warm up the Scotty ... my neck is sore and I want my slippers so I can stand up straight. I keep hitting the ceiling. But I feel good."

The weather was harsh that winter—temperatures dipped below zero one
night and water in the five-gallon jug froze
solid. But throughout the stay, Steve was
upbeat, willing to sacrifice the comforts
of home for the larger, more important
purpose of fixing his beloved society. In a
letter to me he wrote, "Linda I love you as
much as ever. I want you to know that I
feel like there may be purpose and direction in my life now … I have a mission to
do, and although it's very hard for YOU,
I appreciate your allowing me to do this.
And I'll try to do a good job and not piss
off anyone too bad that I get in trouble.
I'm going to have to work now at venting
my anger in a productive way to get Jack
to step down or be taken down."

Torn apart emotionally by a man
who expressed his love while insisting
that his mission against SAE was up-
permost in his life, I felt on the verge of
emotional collapse. Throughout the separation, I slept poorly and cried often to
Nancy about my "half-married, half-sepa-
rated" life.

Steve and I continued to argue

whenever we saw each other, mostly about his not being out of the home when I was there. He frequently stayed at the house until I returned from work, and sometimes spent part of a Saturday working in the garage. It was so like him to overstep the arrangement we'd made, but also so like me to allow these transgressions. I'd adopted the habit of enabling long before the word became part of our everyday language.

"If you want to be out of our lives for two months, then please stay away when you are supposed to," I wrote in one of the many letters we exchanged during this time. "It's emotionally less stressful for me when we're apart. I am torn in your presence; being separate makes me feel quieter inside."

Although I was confused and unhappy, living apart gave me time to think about what I wanted when—or if—he returned. In a rambling ten-page letter composed at four o'clock one morning a month into our separation, I wrote about what I needed if we renewed our relationship. "For the past several years, our focus has been on what we need to do to get you and your work back on track. We've both paid little attention to what I need, what I want out of life, what it takes for me to be happy."

Living separately gave me the space to understand that I was no longer willing to live as I had. I continued: "Our future does not only depend on your ability to let go of SAE, but also on whether we have enough love left to build anew. When I look deep inside me, I know that I can no longer stay married to a man who doesn't share the same values, the same dreams."

During this time, Nancy encouraged me to seek a legal separation, one that would protect me from Steve's unpredictable spending. While in the Scotty, he occasionally spent several hundred dollars at a store, once filling two grocery carts at Wal-Mart. He didn't tell me about these purchases, but they showed up on the credit card bill, which I paid. Nancy worried that his unpredictable buying habits could lead to serious financial trouble if I didn't make our separation legal. I agreed to talk to a lawyer, but never mustered the will to call one.

Steve lived in the Scotty for six
weeks, until leaving for SAE's annual
convention in Detroit. He'd been to the
conference before, but not since he quit
working there. Jack and members of the
board of directors would be in Detroit,
and his best opportunity for advancing
his concerns to a higher level would be
a one-on-one meeting with the president
of SAE's board of directors. He and Steve
had corresponded by mail in the months
leading up to the week-long event, but the
president never agreed to meet with him.
Steve thought he could change his mind
in Detroit.

In hindsight, it is easier to view
Steve's increasing obsession with the engineering society as a symptom of mental
illness, but at the time he remained ami-
able in his dealings with others, especially
when talking about SAE. Even the psychiatrist he saw did not view his fixation
as mania, another indication of the medical community's limited understanding of
mental illness in the mid-1990s. In fact, it
was the psychiatrist who helped hammer

out the specifics of our separation. Her parting words to me when we left her office that Saturday morning were, "Maybe spending two months in a cold camper will make him think twice about what he's doing."

The week before Steve left for Detroit, he asked if John could go with him. John had been to other SAE-sponsored events before, so his request wasn't unusual. But his wanting John there is a window into Steve's intuitive nature when interacting with others. He knew that his image had been marred by his letter-writing campaign against the society, and John's presence would soften the negative impressions he'd made.

Success in Detroit was essential for Steve, for the Ides of March was approaching. With an optimism not tethered to reality, Steve gave little thought to the scale of the task he faced—to remove a respected executive vice president of an international engineering society from office. Nor did Steve think about what might happen if he failed. In a note to me before leaving for the convention, he shared his

unwavering commitment to the cause:
"I've focused on making a change at SAE,
it's taken me over ... If this cannot be
done, I'm in real trouble, because it's the
only thing that needs to be done for me
to want to contribute to society again in a
way that I'm naturally inclined."

While in Detroit, Steve and John
stayed with Steve's cousin. She and her
husband lived about an hour from Cobo
Center, where the convention was held.
For three days Steve and John visited the
various displays and listened to presen-
tations, all while Steve continued in his
effort to arrange a meeting with the board
president. On the fourth day, John stayed
behind to finish school assignments in
anticipation of returning home the next
day, and Steve went alone to the convention center. Seeing Steve without John,
a friend and former SAE colleague cau-
tioned Steve about being in Detroit, saying
that his "presence makes the higher ups
very uncomfortable."

That night, the home phone rang. It
was Steve talking loud and fast.

"I'm being followed," Steve blurted

when I picked up the phone by my bed. It was two in the morning, and the ringing pulled me from a fitful sleep. It took several seconds to register what he was saying; when it did I could hear he was revved and frightened.

"Is John okay?" I asked, and when he didn't answer, I asked again.

"He's fine. He's fine," Steve said dismissively, his voice rising with urgency. "You need to know that people are after me, that I'm being followed."

"What are you talking about? Who's following you?" I asked, trying to make sense of what I was hearing. By now I'm fully awake and in the kitchen heating water for tea.

"The FBI. The Pinkerton police. Cobo security. The Detroit police. They're all watching me."

"You're not making any sense. Why would they be following you?" I interjected, trying to take control of the conversation. Steve's words slowed as he explained how someone from SAE told him that he's been under surveillance since coming to Detroit.

"It all makes sense now," Steve said. "When we were standing in line to register, they took John and me through a separate check-in line. And last night I left Cobo Center so late that the parking garage was closed. I couldn't get my car out so a security guard offered me money for a cab ride home. Why would he offer me money? Then I saw two guys walking on the opposite side of the street watching my every move."

Who would be watching Steve, I wondered as I paced the cold kitchen floor. His explanation seemed far-fetched, fantastical, and I doubted that a security guard would offer him money for a cab.

"The board president finally agreed to meet with me tomorrow," Steve said, "but now I think they're setting me up!" Hearing this, I knew Steve and John wouldn't be coming home as planned.

"You promised to have John home by tomorrow," I said. I'd agreed to John's going as long as he didn't miss too many days of school. I didn't like that Steve was backing down on his promise. But Steve wouldn't talk about that. He was worried about tomorrow's meeting. He continued, "I've been trying for months to get this meeting, and all of sudden he says yes. Why? I know the FBI is following me, and you should know that too. In case something happens at the meeting."

Still frightfully naïve about the nature of mania, I dismissed most of what Steve said. It sounded like a ramped-up version of what I'd been hearing for the past several months: That he wanted to meet with the board president. That Jack had to be removed from office. That SAE must return to its core mission. My default response to these rants had been to shut out what was being said, and I tried doing that. We're separated, I told myself. Let him figure it out. I should focus on getting John away from whatever craziness Steve is involved in.

Several hours later, Steve's cousin called, and I knew the situation was serious.

"I don't think he slept at all last night," she said. "He's been talking non-stop since I got up. When I went to the bathroom to brush my teeth, he followed me there."

She and I agreed to rendezvous later that afternoon at an interstate rest stop
east of Toledo. A neighbor would intercept
Luke and Elly when they got off the school
bus, and another neighbor drove with me
to retrieve John. On the car ride home, he
sat in the back seat and said very little.
I recorded one of his observations in my
journal: "John said he was awake when
Pop got back last night. The first thing he
did was close all the blinds. Then he kept
peeking through them, like someone was
outside."

Steve met with the board president
the next morning, and he encouraged
Steve to give up his efforts against the
engineering society. The president also
called me when he and Steve were together, hoping I could persuade him to come
home. I told the president that I agreed
with him, but there was little I could do
to stop Steve. We're separated, I said, and
Steve was acting on his own. The next
time I heard from Steve, it was from a pay
phone at Detroit's Psychiatric Institute.

"Will you accept the charges?" the

operator asked, and I said, "Yes."

Three days later, Nancy and I were in Detroit, talking to the hospital's social worker, who filled us in on what had happened. Following his unsuccessful meeting with the board president, Steve prowled the corridors of Cobo Center looking for Jack. He was wearing a sweatshirt with the words Caution Bad Ass printed on the back. According to the police report, it took several security guards to subdue him. He was handcuffed and searched and placed in the back seat of a Detroit police car. Later, Steve recounted his conversation with two officers:

"I don't know what to do with you," one of the officers mused, trying to assess the problem with the clean-cut white guy sitting there. "Should I take you to jail or the psych ward?" the officer asked.

Steve refused to be drawn in by his easy-going banter, and the officer asked again. "Would you rather spend the night in a cell or a psych ward?"

Still, Steve said nothing.

"If I take you to the station, they're going to book you," the officer explained.

Finally Steve blurted, "You're the ones who put me here. You can figure out what to do with me."

The social worker at Detroit Psychiatric shared the police report with Nancy and me. It read in part: "Subject ... was going in offices and yelling and screaming saying he was on his final mission. Writer attempted to talk to him and he was calm one minute and hyper yelling about Governor Romney. Officers of SAE stated he has made threats about the vice president of SAE that he was going to take him out."

Steve's calling out for Governor Romney during the rampage is another hint of his muddled thought processes at this time. Steve had corresponded recently via mail with Mr. Romney, who had been president of American Motors Corporations, which built Ramblers. Steve met the former Michigan governor briefly the previous year at a national Rambler meet. Later, Steve sent Mr. Romney a letter, and he answered with a note, which was among the many letters in his SAE box. The night before his breakdown in Detroit, he called Mr. Romney's Michigan home. Steve thought that Mr. Romney might somehow help him in his campaign against SAE.

Chapter 10

Unhinged

"Today is Monday, March 6, 1995, and I am beginning an account of the five most traumatic days of my life. I'm sitting in the waiting room at Detroit Psychiatric Institute where Steve has been since early Friday morning." That's the beginning of a journal entry chronicling the events leading up to Steve's mental breakdown on the final day of SAE's convention.

Rereading those words years later, I see again the dilapidated red brick building and barred windows and smell the musty reception area where Nancy and I sit with Steve. A guard paces the perimeter of the large, cement-block room, watching as a score of mostly men mill about. Two men talk quietly in a corner, and two others bend over a Checkers board at a worn cafeteria table. The three of us sit at another table. People seem curious to see us, two neatly dressed women in their mid-40s visiting a distinguished-looking man in a psychiatric hospital not far from downtown Detroit. Most of the patients wear street clothes, but Steve is in faded hospital garb.

"Why aren't you wearing your clothes?" I ask when we settle in at the table. I keep my voice quiet, as if speaking loudly might compromise the delicate equilibrium of the unfolding drama.

"I'd be easier to spot on the street if I try to escape," he says matter-of-factly, seemingly unaware of the strangeness of his response. He even seems unmindful as to why he's there, when only three days ago he was attending an international engineering conference.

Nancy and I met earlier in the afternoon at a Bob Evans restaurant south of Toledo. She drove from her home in Illinois while I came with Elly from Pennsylvania. I didn't leave immediately after Steve's phone call Friday morning. Instead, I finished up several articles at the newspaper and made arrangements to be away for an extended period. Delaying my departure also allowed Nancy's husband, Mark, who was in California on a work trip, to fly home a day early so he could be with their children. And my sister-in-law Mary Ann traveled from her home in southeastern Ohio to watch John and Luke. John had missed four days of school the previous week, and I wasn't sure how long I'd be gone.

Steve's mother met us at the Bob Evans. She will take Elly to her house while Nancy and I are in Detroit. Steve's father, Fred, and his sister, Joyce, will join us tomorrow, and together we will try and sort out what to do next. As I say good-bye to Elly in the restaurant parking lot, Steve's mother slips a Baggie with several miniature Snickers bars into my coat pocket. "Give these to Steve," she says quietly, her eyes glistening with unshed tears.

Sitting at the cafeteria table with Steve several hours later, I push the candy towards him. His hands tremble as he takes a bar from the bag, then pushes the

Baggie back to me. "I'm not supposed to have plastic," he says solemnly, his voice childlike and innocent. He seems more concerned with breaking a minor hospital infraction than the circumstances that landed him here in the first place. Nancy and I talk while Steve wrestles a piece of candy from its wrapper, his fingers clumsy from the drugs he's taking. He asks no questions and offers little explanation as to what happened. Not wanting to agitate, I don't push for particulars. Our conversation bumps along awkwardly, and I fill the silence with the minutia of our lives: Elly is staying with Grandma Schmitmeyer; Mary Ann is watching the boys; I drove to Michigan in the Pontiac earlier that morning; his Dad and sister, Joyce, will visit tomorrow. I'm not sure of how much he understands or even cares about what I am saying; he is focused solely on the candy before him.

When an attendant announces that visiting hours are over, Steve stands quickly to comply. Steve has always been eager to please others, and according to his parents, readily did whatever was asked of him. His father loves telling how as a little boy Steve sat patiently with the old men at the grain elevator on Saturday mornings listening to their stories while he unloaded the wheat or corn from the hopper wagon. Steve's mother always adds, "When Steve was only four, he got a nickel from a man in the pew next to him for being good at Mass."

As we stand to leave, Steve cups one hand to the edge of the table and with the other clumsily gathers the stray crumbs from the scuffed tabletop. Looking for a trashcan, he spots one across the open room and walks stiffly towards it, cradling the candy wrappers and crumbs in his right hand while the other lies limp at his side. His feet brush the worn speck-led linoleum as he walks. Swish, swish, swish, like a robot. The "Haldol shuffle," I will learn later, ape-like movements caused by the antipsychotic medication he's taking. Placing the wrappers in the trashcan, he turns to leave. When I realize that he's not even going to say good-bye, I touch his arm to slow his progress.

"May I have a kiss?" I ask.

Bending down, he brushes his dry lips against mine. It has been two months since we have been this close, and I'm taken aback at the flatness of our exchange. Tears well in my eyes as he turns to go. Nancy and I walk arm-in-arm down a long dark corridor, and my tears flow freely. Putting her arm around me, Nancy pulls me close, and I bend my head to her shoulder. The setting sun casts a long, solitary shadow of the two of us as we make our way to the parking lot.

The next morning, Nancy and I meet with Steve's caseworker. He's a tall, thin man wearing rumpled khakis and a soft blue open-collared shirt. His office is in a remote section of the institute and sparsely furnished with a desk and several straight-back chairs. There are other desks in this makeshift office, but no one else is here. The caseworker is soft-spoken; he projects an aura of empathy when he talks.

"Your husband's situation is different from most of the cases here," he says, an apparent nod to the bewilderment I feel at finding Steve locked up in an inner-city psych ward. According to the admissions report, he says, Steve was brought in by the Detroit police late Thursday night following a scuffle at Cobo Center. He explains that first he was taken to a holding area of the hospital, where he had to be strapped to the bed. He'd been yelling at the staff, repeatedly telling them that he was "just an old farm boy." The only way to quiet him was a strong sedative.

Later, Steve shared details of the incident. "Five hospital attendants stood around my bed. One of them was carrying a long needle. I saw what they did to another patient, so I started bucking. Four guys held me down, but I just kept moving so they couldn't get the needle in. Then the woman said, 'I don't think we're going to be able to do this.' I relaxed a little, and she jabbed me in the butt."

Steve awoke twelve hours later. Chafed wrists and a bruised bottom were the only visible signs of his late-night interaction with the hospital orderlies. The emotional scars, however, lingered for a long time.

"Your husband has been placed on

a 5150," the caseworker says, explaining that it's an involuntary commitment that is effective for up to seventy-two hours. Steve has the option of signing himself into another hospital or being made a ward of the state. If he stays at Detroit Psychiatric, he will have a court hearing within ten days and be committed for another thirty to sixty days, depending on what the court doctor deems necessary.

"Most of the patients aren't like your husband," the caseworker says again. "Our goal here is to stabilize Steve so he won't be a danger to himself or others."

I get the sense that he's trying to tell me something, but I don't know exactly what. This is all woefully unfamiliar to me, and I look to Nancy, hoping she understands what he's suggesting. As a physical therapist, Nancy has always been there when I needed medical advice. But this is different from a child with a high temperature or a sprained ankle. Isn't stabilizing him what we want? Is he suggesting Steve not be kept here?

The caseworker continues: "No

charges have been filed against him, so he can be treated elsewhere. If he goes to another hospital, though, I'm required to notify the FBI."

"The FBI?" I say, stunned.

Thinking he made a mistake, I say, "You mean the Detroit police," for certainly the FBI wasn't involved in such a minor infraction.

"They filed a report too," the caseworker says, "but the FBI report has to be passed on to whatever facility treats him."

I shake my head in disbelief. Steve involved with the FBI? It seems utterly impossible. Until recently, he's been the most easy-going and non-confrontational man I knew, friendly and forthright in the extreme. Others thought so, too. What about that silly trophy he got at Wright-Patterson for being the league's "friendliest bowler." And just yesterday, when we visited Steve in the hospital, he introduced Nancy and me to a number of the patients he'd made friends with in the short time he was there. He's been strangely different, I know, but nothing on a scale that would involve the FBI.

"Some of the letters he sent to SAE staff were considered threatening," the caseworker explains. "It's a federal offense to send threats through the U.S. mail, so the FBI was brought in."

"Really?" I say, the pieces of a puzzle beginning to fit together in my mind. "So that's why he's had to let headquarters know when he was going there." For the past six months Steve has had to notify SAE whenever he planned to visit someone there or to use the society's library, which he did occasionally.

"Yes," the caseworker says. "An FBI agent from the Pittsburgh office is at headquarters whenever Steve is there. And when Steve registered for the convention, the Pittsburgh office notified the Detroit office. He's been under surveillance since he arrived."

The caseworker also tells us that Jack has had a bodyguard while at the conference. Reading the police officer's report, I see their concerns, for it refers to Steve's "strong military association" and "expertise in weaponry," which, the report says, he acquired through fourteen years as a civilian engineer at Wright-Patterson Air Force Base. The report seems exaggerated, but clearly they're not taking a chance now that he's locked up.

• • •

The following day, Steve was transferred to St. Rita's Hospital in Lima, Ohio, where he spent the next month. The psychiatrist he'd been seeing in Pittsburgh didn't have hospital privileges, and Steve's sister, Joyce, knew a doctor at St. Rita's who would take him as a new patient. She and her family live near Lima, as do both Steve's and my parents and other family members. They will be able to visit regularly while I am in Pennsylvania, working and caring for the children.

The decision to transfer Steve to St. Rita's instead of leaving him at Detroit Psychiatric wasn't easy. None of the people helping me decide really understood how to deal with someone with a mental illness. In a journal entry written several weeks after returning to Pennsylvania, I wrote:

Steve's father and sister came
to Detroit to visit on Monday.
After they saw him, they met
with Nancy and me in the
hospital lobby where we talked for a long time about what
we should do. It's also where
we almost made the biggest
mistake about Steve's care.
All of us agreed that if Steve
were transferred to St. Rita's
and was nearer to family and
friends, he may not work
hard at getting better, and
that he would slip into his
old habit of making a social
situation out of his medical
stay. We thought of Steve's
condition more as an inherent
weakness in his character.

When we told the psychiatrist
of our decision to keep Steve
in Detroit, he simply asked,
"Have you seen where he's
been staying?" We hadn't,
and I'm sure he was referring
to the horrors of that hospital...

The psychiatrist then told us
that his goal was to stabilize Steve. He added that in
group therapy Steve would

be a model for others, but
his intelligence and ability to
understand the illness was
essential to his getting better,
and that he had far more ad-
vantages than the others who
would be with him in group
therapy.

My journal entry reflects the limited understanding we had of how to treat
mental illness. We thought that keeping
Steve in Detroit would force him to come
to his senses about his obsession with
SAE. None of us knew then that a mental
illness diagnosis requires the same supportive and caring environment as any
other illness, and the patient deserves the
best treatment available.

My journal entry continued: "In retrospect, what really makes me shudder is
how close we came to leaving him in Detroit. How wrong it would have been. But
we simply didn't understand how to deal
with him. In our defense I can only say
that we kept our minds open, listening to
what his doctor had to say."

Keeping an open mind to the many
changes that lie ahead was at the crux

of my eventually coming to terms with Steve's illness. A disorder that affects the degree of control a person has over his thoughts and behaviors was beyond my understanding then. I was embarking on a steep learning curve, one that would take years to work through and a lifetime to understand.

Steve spent two weeks as an inpatient at St. Rita's and two weeks in Day Hospital, where he began the years-long process of learning what it meant to live with a severe mental illness. The lengthy hospital stay allowed time for doctors to adjust the dosage of his psychotropic drugs, some of which took weeks to be fully effective. The children and I visited every weekend, and with each trip I saw a more modulated husband and father. When he was discharged from the hospital, he was taking five different medications: lithium, to stabilize his mood; Ativan, for anxiety; Haldol, to counter the psychotic thinking that often occurs during a severe manic episode; Wellbutrin, an antidepressant; and Artane, a sedative. I write this now with an enhanced under-

standing of these drugs, though at the
time, they were merely a litany of words
that held little meaning.

Although traumatic, Steve's breakdown initially brought a sense of relief to
our family life. Bipolar disorder, or manic
depression as it was called then, seemed
like a clear-cut medical diagnosis, a
chemical imbalance in the brain, not just
low moods brought on by the series of job
changes several years earlier. It was treatable, a medical problem that Steve and I
would face together.

None of us knew then, not even the
doctors who treated him, that it would
take another three years before Steve was
mentally stable. The delusional thinking
Steve experienced about SAE was not a
temporary condition associated with the
onset of the disorder, but chronic, one
treatable with antipsychotic medication.
Steve's psychosis, his steadfast fixation
on the engineering society, would resurface six months after leaving St. Rita's,
after he had been weaned from Haldol.
Without the antipsychotic drug, episodes
would occur occasionally for several more

years, until the medical community better understood the specific nature of Steve's illness.

Three months after leaving to live in the Scotty, Steve came home, driving the '64 Rambler station wagon he and John took to Michigan, the upside down "Why be normal?" sticker still in the back window. Nestled on the front seat next to him was a six-week-old Jack Russell Terrier, a surprise gift for the kids from Joyce and her husband.

Three years younger than Steve, Joyce has always been close to her brother. She followed him to the University of Dayton, where she studied art education. Steve's younger sister, Jenny, also graduated from UD, in mechanical engineering. Steve was seventeen when Jenny was born, and only later, as adults, did they become close. Steve and Joyce lived together several years after graduating from college, until Steve and I married. Now Joyce and her family live on a horse farm near Lima, where Steve stayed when he was in Day Hospital. Joyce and I talked by phone every day. That's when we decided it would be a good idea for Steve to bring a puppy when he returned home.

Since moving to Pennsylvania, our family has frequently made the five-hour drive across northern Ohio. But when Steve was discharged from St. Rita's, his father said he would follow Steve in his own car. The drugs Steve took were sedating, and he often seemed disconnected from what was going on around him. Knowing Fred, though, I also thought he wanted to make sure Steve went home, and not to the Scotty, which was still parked by our friend's barn. My suspicion was confirmed the next morning when, before returning to Ohio, Fred insisted on wrestling the camper from the muddy farm field before he left.

Both Steve's and my family supported us in many ways after Steve's breakdown, although, like me, they didn't really understand what was happening. My mother, widowed unexpectedly when she was sixty, also visited occasionally, mostly to care for the children and help out around the house.

Steve's parents helped too. For the

first few follow-up visits with the psychiatrist in Lima, Fred went with him. He didn't just meet Steve at St. Rita's, a forty-five minute drive from their home. Instead he drove to our house and then back to Lima with Steve, who for the first several months remained too compromised to go alone. These trips were no small undertaking for a man in his early 70s.

Yet, despite their continued helpfulness, Steve's parents seemed reluctant to openly accept that their son had a mental illness. German, Catholic, and children of the Depression, they deeply valued one's ability to work hard, something Steve no longer was able to do. Frequently, when Fred and Steve worked together on a house project while they visited, I'd hear Fred telling Steve that he just had to set his mind to getting better and to "pull yourself up by your bootstraps," one of Fred's favorite phrases. They also were reluctant to talk about the illness, even when Steve tried talking with them about it. They weren't unlike the many who shy away from the subject. But their doing so unintentionally added to the isolation

Steve and I felt.

I was frequently frustrated and angry during this time by the silence that surrounded Steve's illness. Throughout Steve's long hospital stay, only a handful of people visited him, despite our many friends and relatives in the area. And he received only a half-dozen get-well cards. I understood why, but it still hurt. This general lack of support contrasted sharply to the many well wishes Steve received six years later when he underwent surgery for prostate cancer. In one note I received while Steve was at St. Rita's, a friend who happens to be a nurse wrote kindheartedly of her concern and then added, "I won't be sharing details about Steve with anyone." Although she meant no harm, her message reinforced my own misunderstanding, that somehow what happened was shameful. It took years for Steve and me to transcend the stigma of mental illness, but as we better understood the nature of mental disorders, we grew confident in talking about it.

The first time Steve openly shared his diagnosis occurred more than two

years after his breakdown, and it was
with a stranger on a plane. The two of
us were coming home from the National
Alliance on Mental Illness (NAMI) convention in Albuquerque. I'd visited the local
NAMI chapter while Steve was still in the
hospital, and through the next couple of
years actively participated in programs
sponsored by the mental health advocacy
organization. Steve regularly attended
local NAMI support group meetings and
participated in several research trials
at the Stanley Center for the Innovative
Treatment of Bipolar Disorder, then part
of the University of Pittsburgh's Department of Psychiatry. We also participated
in NAMI workshops and conferences in
the Pittsburgh area. Then the local NAMI
chapter sponsored our trip to Albuquerque. The convention theme that year was
fighting the stigma of mental illnesses.
More than 2,000 family members, health-
care providers, researchers, and people
with mental illnesses were there. Being
surrounded by so many who understood
what we were going through was a pivotal
experience for both of us. On the plane

home, Steve struck up a conversation with a well-dressed young woman seated next to him. When she asked why we were in Albuquerque, he explained our participation in the convention, making sure she understood what NAMI stood for.

"Are you a doctor?" the woman asked.

"No," Steve said. "I have a mental illness."

His reply was a milestone of sort, another step in the long road to understanding and living with a mental disorder.

• • •

Standing at the island counter, I see Steve's and Fred's cars pull into the driveway. "Your father's home," I call, and by the time Steve reaches the front door, the kids and I are in the kitchen waiting. Running to her father, six-year-old Elly spots the small animal he cradles in his hands. "Daddy's got a puppy. Daddy's got a puppy," she cries, and all eyes turn to the six-week-old animal nestled in the palm of Steve's hand.

The children are looking at the puppy, but I am watching Steve. Although I saw him every weekend while he was in the hospital, he seems greatly changed standing in the entranceway of our home. He's rounder in the face and thicker in the middle. Weight gain is a side effect of several of the medications he takes, but he looks almost obese. Far heavier than the 32-inch waistline he had during most of our years together.

"Can we keep it?" Luke wants to know, pulling me from my thoughts.

"It's a gift from Joyce," I say, "for all of you." Catching Luke's eye, I mouth, "Especially for you."

It's been four months since Luke's accident, and he's still the most out-wardly angry about what's happened. A semblance of his earlier life has re-turned—he's back in school and playing ice hockey. But he still craves what most middle schoolers want—what I wanted at his age—a family that blends seamlessly with his friends' families. The past year has been anything but that.

Spot—the name Steve gives the puppy because of the large tan mark on her back—becomes the focal point of Steve's long-awaited homecoming. Soon everyone is seated around the island counter, as we've done so many times before. I'm standing in my usual place on the "working" side of the counter. From here I see again the tableau of my family: The three kids sit on stools, squabbling over Spot as she waddles back and forth between them. Grandpa sits at the periphery of our family circle, making endless banter with his grandchildren, straining to achieve an illusion of normalcy. Steve is on a stool too, but in his own world. He seems unaware of the commotion around him. When he lifts a glass to take a drink of milk, his hand trembles.

Recovering from a psychotic episode is a long, slow process. Steve's mind and appearance are greatly altered, and I don't know if this is because of the breakdown or the medications he takes. I asked those who might know—Steve's doctor and therapist, people in support groups, even the woman at the local NAMI chapter whose

husband has bipolar disorder—as I try to
understand the changes I see. For a long
time everything feels uncertain, gray, the
color of smoke, where sickness and health
intersect.

For the children and me, the long
slow road to recovering from what has
happened over the past several months
will involve understanding and accepting
a changed father and husband. For Steve,
it will require reimagining himself and
finding a new way forward. For he is no
longer who he once was—cheerful, confident, carefree, the provider for his growing
family. Like the illness that crept unsus-
pectingly into our lives over several years,
the return to normalcy will be equally
long—and even more arduous.

Hanging above the dresser mirror
in Steve's and my bedroom more than two
decades after Detroit is a kindergarten
art project Elly made that year. I've kept
it as a reminder of the many challenges
our family faced then. It's a simple project, one to help children understand the
ending of one year and the beginning of
the next. To make it, she traced the num-

bers 1-9-9-5 onto a white sheet of paper and outlined them in red and gold glitter. Matting the numbers on green construction paper, she fashioned a hanger from yellow yarn. The sign "1995," minus some of the glitter, still hangs in our bedroom. That year was a turning point for our family, where the past no longer served as a guide for the future. For me, it was the beginning of learning to accept that which was, and not what I thought should be. And to love anew a husband who bore little resemblance to the vibrant, smiling man who reached out to me at the skating rink so many years ago.

Chapter 11

Bird by Bird

"When is Lukie coming home?" Elly asks repeatedly on a Saturday morning in July, sixteen months after Steve's return. The two of us are in the kitchen gathering supplies for an overnight camping trip in the Scotty, and she's anxious to get going. Luke, twelve, slept at a friend's house last night, and his friend's mother is dropping him off this morning. The two boys went skating at a nearby ice rink, a favorite Friday night hangout for middle school boys and girls. Both Luke and John skate there often, as does Luke's friend, who is also on the middle school ice hockey team. He likes teasing Luke about being good at skating backwards because of all the practice he gets talking to the girls on Friday night.

This is our first trip in the camper since Steve and his father pulled it from the farmer's field when he came home from the hospital. We are headed to a campground ninety minutes west of our home, just into eastern Ohio. Elly loves the idea of sleeping in the Scotty, which is parked on the cement pad outside our house. Everything about it is small, a perfect playhouse for a seven-year-old. When we camped regularly, I kept it stocked with supplies, but we haven't used it since Steve returned. There's a lot of getting ready for one night of camping. John is helping Steve strap the boys' bikes to the back of the camper and load firewood into the station wagon. Elly assists too, carrying out bedding and bags of groceries.

The camper was once a focal point of our family's summer activity. We used it frequently at nearby tractor shows and state parks. When the kids were little, we all slept in it, Steve in the single bed, and Luke and I in the double. John slept in a hammock above the double mattress, and Elly, still used to sleeping in a crib, slept in the 3- by 3-foot well at the center of the camper. I think of the Scotty as a metal tent on wheels, where we stay dry when it rains, mostly. It leaks around the back window and in one corner, where the sheet metal has separated. Now that the boys are older, and bigger, they'll sleep in a pup tent, and Steve, Elly, and I will share the Scotty.

• • •

I got interested in camping after graduating from college. It's an inexpensive way to travel, and I like how living outdoors strips daily routines of their convenience. It makes habit elemental, forcing a person to focus on process instead of getting things done. I'm goal-oriented to a fault, and my workload has exacerbated this tendency. A night of camping might help me relax. After graduating from the university, I spent three summers with my college friend crisscrossing the United States and Canada in my Volkswagen van. She was a teacher too, and the two of us headed out shortly after the last day of class and returned in time for the next school year.

Those trips were my first real travel adventures. When I was growing up, family outings involved Sunday afternoon visits to cousins in the next county. There was also our family's annual half-day vacation to Lake Loramie, a small manmade lake twenty minutes from our house. Mom was usually up by 3 a.m. to fry chicken and pack the coolers so we could be at the lake in time to watch the sun rise. My parents packed a day's worth of food and fun into those brief getaways—from cooking breakfast outdoors to fishing, swimming, and playing baseball. We were back home by late-afternoon, though, so my brothers could deliver the papers on their newspaper routes. We kids called it vacation, and it was an adventurous, carefree day, unlike the purposeful manner in which we lived our lives.

One of the things that attracted me to Steve was his family's sense of adventure. Even though he grew up on a dairy farm in the 1950s—a time when most people and even fewer farmers took time off from their everyday lives—his family was often on the go. If inclement weather prevented them from working outside after they finished the morning milking, they left for a day trip to the city. They'd shop in a department store and eat at a restaurant, then be back home in time for the evening milking. They also spent Sunday afternoons waterskiing and, in the winter, playing pick-up ice hockey on Fort Loramie lake. Steve was as adept at skiing as he was at skating, and when I met him, he, like Luke, loved impressing the girls. There's a high school picture of him slaloming behind his father's boat, tanned and smiling brightly, the towrope hooked to the heel of his foot while two-handing a heavy wooden ski high above his head.

The Schmitmeyers also took real family vacations, once to Florida in the winter, and when Steve turned seven, annually to a fishing camp near Rice Lake in Ontario. I was drawn to his family's robust sense of play, and when Steve and I first married, we followed suit, with biennual trips to Rice Lake and camping vacations with Nancy and her family throughout the eastern United States. Steve and I also traveled to Europe and South America shortly after we married, and when he was with SAE, to a committee meeting in Moscow.

I loved the adventuresome life we had together. Now, though, as I watch my family getting ready for an overnight camping trip, the travel excitement I once felt feels long ago and far away. My wings have been clipped, and every day is a lesson in learning to live life differently than I'd imagined.

• • •

After setting up camp, I stretch out on a lawn chair by a stream, alone for what feels like the first time in months. When Steve first suggested a trip in the Scotty, I resisted because of the work involved. I have little energy for extras now, and an overnight in the camper didn't seem worth the effort. But Steve persisted and I agreed, especially since he promised me time for myself once we got there. Steve is aware of the imbalance of responsibilities in our relationship. Whether he's capable of doing more is something we both wrestle with. "I'm a worn-out woman," I say frequently, trying for a light-hearted tone, even though it isn't always there. He tries helping when he's not low. But his abilities are limited. He can no longer juggle multiple thoughts, holding one idea in his head while acting on another. His doctor says he has problems with his working and short-term memory. But no one can say whether it's from the drugs or the disorder. Like when we were getting ready. I reminded him to bring a load of firewood and the big red and yellow water jug we use for drinking water. He remembered the firewood but forgot the jug. I pay close attention to everything he does, lest something be overlooked. But despite his limitations, he remains the thoughtful man he always was, and after setting up camp and eating lunch, he tells me he and Elly are going for a walk. The boys have already left on their bikes to explore the grounds. Sitting here by the stream, I watch Steve and Elly make their way along a rocky creek bank leading to the lake.

I pick up a book to read and know immediately it isn't going to happen. Escaping into a good book doesn't work anymore. My mind won't slow sufficiently to be absorbed by a story. Besides, there won't be time to finish it when I'm at home. Instead, I take out several sheets of paper from my tote bag. At the top of the first page I write, "Things I Do."

The journal writing I do throughout Steve's illness isn't always neat, chronological entries in a bound book, although I have several of those. It's more snatches of thoughts and feelings written on a yellow legal paper. Today I decide to list everything I feel responsible for, from my job at the newspaper to cooking and cleaning and caring for our children and our home. The act of writing is a way of discharging the angst that comes from living with a man who has a mental illness. I'm not sure what I'll do with what I've written, but I like the feel of my hand moving across the yellow pad. It helps me feel less angry.

I began using yellow tablets after attending a reading by the poet Maya Angelou, who said she used them when she wrote. At the reading, she shared a poem and talked about her life. Growing up in the South in the 1930s, Angelou was mute for several years after being raped as a child. She was a troubled young adult, eventually moving to California in the 1950s with her infant son. Desperate and "mad as hatter," as she described herself, she sought out her former voice teacher who'd also moved to California. The teacher gave her a yellow pad of paper and told her to write down her blessings. Angelou protested, saying she couldn't imagine how she was blessed. The teacher persisted. He reminded her that she was able to speak, that she could see the yellow paper she held in her hands, that she could write. "Before I reached the bottom of the page, I was transformed," Angelou told the audience, words that echo within as I write on my yellow pad.

I'm drawn to others who face life challenges through writing. My own great-great-great grandmother was a writer. Her writings are compiled in a book called *Liwwät Böke, 1807-1882, Pioneer*, pub-

lished by a local Ohio historical society.
She wrote about everyday life in the mid-
19th century. She also drew pictures on
the sheaves of paper she brought with her
from Germany. She told of her passage
to America and the challenges of farming
the dark wooded lands of western Ohio.
She also wrote of the loneliness she and
other frontier women experienced as they
settled into life far from their extended
families. And she told of the death of her
only daughter at the age of fifteen.

Liwwät emigrated to the German
Catholic community of St. John's, about a
half-hour from where Steve and I grew up.
Like most pioneers' lives, Liwwät's was
filled with hardship. Of her six children,
only three lived to maturity. In the prime
of their life together, her husband, Natz,
fell from a tree and broke his hip and
back. He was confined to a bed until his
death three years later. Despite her hard
life—or maybe because of it—she continued to write and draw for more than seven
decades, until her death in 1882.

In one passage she explained why
she spent precious time documenting ev-

eryday life. She listed a dozen reasons; the one that resonates with me is: "Perhaps in twenty, thirty, or ninety years my children's children will come to read my writings ... and they will better understand who they are, and will know that Natz and I were really living persons."

Maybe that's why I write throughout Steve's illness, so that one day I can share my experience with others. So that one day people will better understand the struggles that ordinary people face when someone they love has a severe mental illness.

• • •

On the Things I Do list, I write about paying bills and monitoring finances, attending teachers' conferences and taking Tae Kwon Do. Luke started martial arts lessons several years ago, but the youth center that sponsored the free program requires an adult participate. Steve did it for a while but now says he no longer "feels like it." So reluctantly I'm learning Tae Kwon Do alongside Luke.

I also include on my list "troubleshoot-
ing a problem with the dishwasher" and
"watching a leak in the furnace room so
it doesn't get worse." I write down more
than one hundred things. Toward the
end of the list, when my thoughts turn
to managing Steve's illness, tears well in
my eyes. Still, I continue: "working with
Steve's doctor to understand his illness,"
"comforting Steve when he's low," and,
finally, "passing on information about
Steve's illness so the kids can better un-
derstand/tolerate it."

Since Steve's breakdown, I struggle
daily to understand why he is unable to
participate in life as he once did. That
even though outwardly he appears to be
as he once was, he's no longer responsible
for himself or for our family. This past
year has been one of shifting perceptions,
of letting go of my earlier sense of family to reimagining "us" with a father and
husband who has a serious, chronic, and
difficult to understand illness. I frequently
make reference to Steve being sick when
talking to the children, framing my com-
ments with "because Daddy is sick" and

"it's part of his illness." Saying these things helps me believe them. Given my earlier understanding of the degree of control I thought people had over themselves, it's challenging to accept a husband who obsessively follows his own interest while paying little heed to our needs. I know he should avoid stressful situations, but does that mean I must do everything while he does almost nothing? Is that what the rest of my life will be?

Despite my uncertainty about his illness, I look for opportunities to reinforce the children's understanding that their father is different now. Shortly after he came home from the hospital, I asked Elly if she understood that her father was sick, even though he didn't have a fever or upset stomach, symptoms a six-year-old would comprehend. At the time, she was feeding the fish Steve had bought after Luke's eye accident. I'd made that part of her daily chores, in part because she wanted to feed them but also because I knew she'd follow through. I even made a chart on which she checked the days she fed them.

"I know Daddy is sick because when I feed the fish and ask him what day it is so I can mark it off, he doesn't know anymore," she said, a comment I recorded in my journal.

I've encouraged the children to talk about their father's disorder. I remember John's excitement when he told me about a segment on ABC's "Prime Time Live" in which a reporter interviewed one of President Clinton's speechwriters, who had bipolar disorder. After hearing him tell me about it, I wrote in my journal, "John is like me; he thrives on information about BP."

Coming to terms with the changes in his father was especially difficult for Luke, who, like me, struggled with strong feelings of unfairness. Luke's understanding would come later, and he shared his newly discovered awareness with me in an e-mail when he was a freshman in college. He'd just seen *A Beautiful Mind*, a movie about Nobel Laureate Jonathan Nash's struggle with schizophrenia. Luke had been diagnosed with attention deficit hyperactivity disorder (ADHD) in grade

school, and he likened his inability to concentrate to Steve's lack of control over his
moods and behaviors. He wrote:

> I just wish that I could fig-
> ure out what makes me able
> to concentrate sometimes
> and at other times no matter
> what I do I just can't. I guess
> that frustration is kind of like
> what Pop has to go through
> each day ... I do wish that it
> would not have taken me so
> long to recognize that it was
> something that he could not
> control. I still remember the
> first time that I felt so sorry
> for him instead of being mad.
> It was when we were camping
> out West and he was laying
> in the green tent on the green
> air mattress. For the first
> time, I felt so bad for him.
> After all those years and all
> the times that I was mad at
> him when I should have real-
> ized that it was not his fault. I
> think that was the day that I
> finally started to open myself
> up to new ways of looking at
> (his illness).

The gradual change in the chil-

dren's perception of their father is also
evident in how they addressed him. In
their younger years, John and Luke always called Steve "Pop," something he
encouraged because it sounded more old-
fashioned; it was what his dad called his
father. What is probably more unusual is
that both boys called me Linda, a name I
didn't discourage, maybe because it felt
unique. Steve always called me Linda,
and when John started to talk, he did too.
The name stuck, and when we moved to
Pennsylvania, there were a few side looks
from people who thought I was the children's stepmother. John was seven then,
and once tried explaining our names to a
neighbor: "Pop and Linda aren't their real
names," John said. "It's Steve and Mom."
Elly, influenced by other children at the
babysitter, always called Steve "Daddy."

What's interesting, though, is how
the boys and even I began using the name
Daddy as their father's mental health deteriorated, more endearing and less au-
thoritative than the traditional Pop. This
unconscious shift in language seemed to
reflect the children's increasing aware-

ness of their father's changing role in our family. Steve became "Daddy" to John and Luke for several years, until his mind stabilized again. Then, unwittingly and again over a period of several years, they began calling him Pop again.

Sitting on my lawn chair with my Things I Do list, I think about the challenges of the previous year. Steve isn't any better. For the first several months after Detroit, we were hopeful because there was a clear-cut medical diagnosis, bipolar disorder instead of the vague-sounding situational depression. He's actually worse now, even though he's trying hard to get better. He attends support group meetings and sees a psychiatrist and a therapist regularly. He's been weaned from three of his medications but still takes a mood stabilizer and antidepressant. His doctor took him off the antipsychotic Haldol about six months after leaving the hospital; it was prescribed to counteract the paranoia and erratic thoughts that often occur in the initial stage of bipolar disorder. It's a strong drug with an array of serious side effects,

especially if taken for a long time, specifically tardive dyskinesia, an irreversible
neurological disorder that causes involuntary movements of the tongue, lips, face,
or trunk.

One of the less dangerous but more
annoying side effects is pacing. The Haldol
Shuffle. For the first several weeks after
Steve returned home, he circled the island
counter in the kitchen endlessly, lost into
himself. As the months passed and the
weather warmed, he began pacing around
the perimeter of the cement pad at the
front of our house. Round and round he'd
go, his eyes locked on a spot several feet
in front of him. I liked teasing him sometimes by standing just outside his range
of vision, waiting for him to reach me.
He was always surprised to see me and
would laugh in his old familiar way. A bit-
tersweet moment of togetherness.

It's been almost eighteen months
since Steve's breakdown, and it will be another eighteen months before his psychiatrist finds a combination of medications
that will stabilize his mind, something
I didn't know when I sat by the stream

writing my to-do list. In those intervening
months, doctors will prescribe more than
a dozen different medications or supple-
ments, most with significant side effects:
from twitchy legs to palsied hands, from
loose bowels to listless staring. One drug
will make him fidgety, causing him to pull
at his face and wring his hands. Another
will cause lethargy, and he will sit in his
recliner all day. One will relax him to the
point that his mouth hangs open. "Close
your mouth," I'll snap, the sight of what
looks like a half-witted husband too much
to bear at the end of a long workday.

What baffled doctors in the mid-
1990s was that the paranoia and psychotic thoughts Steve experienced didn't
abate, but were a chronic condition that
needed to be managed with antipsychotic
medication. His fixation with the engineering society would resurface off and
on during the next year-and-a-half, until
the doctor prescribed Risperdal, a newer
antipsychotic drug with fewer side effects.
When that happened, Steve's psychotic
flare-ups finally faded and his diagnosis changed again, to schizoaffective, a

disorder that has some of the symptoms of schizophrenia (paranoia, delusions, and/or disorganized thinking,) and of mood disorders (mania and depression). Schizoaffective was an emerging diagnosis at the time, not fully understood by many practicing psychiatrists. It's common to misdiagnose people with schizoaffective disorder because psychotic symptoms often occur at the onset of bipolar disorder. In Steve's case, though, they never went away—until he was put back on an antipsychotic medication.

In the months since Detroit, I've been working hard to understand Steve's disorder. I go with him to many of his doctor's appointments, and I've joined a support group for those who live with a loved one's mental illness. I also attended a twelve-week information course sponsored by NAMI that was extremely helpful in understanding how changes in personality are the result of a medical condition. And even though I know Steve can't always control his symptoms, I'm frequently angry and unkind. I wish I didn't feel this way, but sometimes I can't help myself.

Despite my efforts, Steve still isn't doing well. He has trouble focusing, whether doing a simple car repair or composing a letter to a Plasquip customer. He's been back in the home office since his breakdown, trying to make a go of it. But he's talking about SAE again, telling his therapist that he feels thwarted at not being able to bring the issue to a close. He rarely talks openly to me about it, but I see how it festers in him. But that was the condition I placed on our being together: No more SAE.

I feel myself drifting further from Steve since Detroit, creating an emotional detachment that allows me to do what a caregiver has to do without feeling so much pain. Instead of sharing the same bed, I sometimes pull a thick foam mattress that we keep beneath our bed and sleep on it. The physical separation helps. Steve doesn't seem to notice. The drugs, or maybe the disorder, make him less aware of these subtleties. I know taking care of Steve is my duty. I've said this to my therapist many times. With Nancy's encouragement and financial support, I've been seeing a counselor off and on since Steve's breakdown. Mostly we talk about coping with the multitude of changes brought about by his illness: its effects on the children, the challenges of living with less money, my feelings of loss, and the illusion of having a partner who's not really there for me. In one visit I shared how walling off my feelings about Steve made life easier. When I said this, the therapist asked what I wanted from my relationship with Steve.

"I could never leave someone who is sick," I said quickly.

I knew that wasn't what she asked, but her question was too scary to think about. Instead I dug deeper into my resolve to stand by Steve. "You wouldn't leave someone who has cancer," I added.

I'm also learning to live more in the moment, to think less about the way things were and more about how they are. I repeatedly tell myself that I want to get to the end of all this without becoming bitter. It's a mantra of sorts, a phrase that focuses my thoughts on what is before me. But I don't know any more whether I can stay with Steve and not become bitter.

I'm reminded of a passage from one of Anne Lamott's books, *Bird by Bird*, in which she talks about her ten-year-old brother being faced with a book report about birds he's put off doing for months. She writes: "He was at the kitchen table close to tears, surrounded by binder paper and pencils and unopened books on birds, immobilized by the hugeness of the task ahead. Then my father sat down beside him, put his arm around my brother's shoulder, and said, 'Bird by bird, buddy. Just take it bird by bird.'"

That's what I try to do. Take it day by day. Even moment by moment. Many times I fail to keep my focus and become overwhelmed by the hugeness of this challenge. But there are also times when I allow whatever I'm doing to consume me. When I become absorbed by the moment. When I feel myself physically move through space, lifting each leg and moving my body forward as I make my way through each day. When I'm able to do this, my legs feel strong and solid. Powerful. Intentionally I place one foot in front of the other. I'm in control of my movement. At these times I'm okay. Bird by bird, I say. Another mantra that keeps me by his side.

Surrounded by quiet and calmed by the act of writing, I watch Steve and Elly as they make their way back to our campsite. Elly bounces from boulder to boulder while Steve steps hesitantly across the rocks. She's holding a bouquet of wildflowers, and Steve is carrying a small, galvanized bucket of "pretty rocks" that Elly has gathered. When they are closer, I see that Steve is tired, worn down by the walk.

Elly scampers to the camper to get a glass for the flowers, and I ask Steve what's wrong. "Didn't you enjoy the walk?"

"It's frustrating," he says. "I can't even keep up with my seven-year-old daughter."

Since his breakdown, Steve has complained often about his lack of coordination. Ten pounds heavier than he was a year ago, he's always been fairly light on his feet. He's no longer sure-footed; he says he has to concentrate going down a set of steps. He's told the psychiatrist and therapist about this, but neither is sure of the cause.

Steve recently read *An Unquiet Mind*, a book about bipolar disorder written by the clinical psychologist Kay Jamison about her struggles with the disorder. She was diagnosed ten years before Steve, and she writes in her book about no longer being able to read for extended periods of time, something that had been part of her everyday life. She was unable to finish a book for ten years, she writes, until she stopped taking lithium. Steve still takes the mood stabilizer, as well as an antidepressant. Since he's only on two meds, we are trying to pinpoint the different side effects. The drugs seem to cause drowsiness, hand tremors, weight gain, less interest in sex, frequent urination, and dry mouth. He wonders if they also cause his lack of coordination and muddled thinking. Like Jamison, he's unable to complete tasks that were once easy. Earlier this summer I watched him struggle to calculate the gas mileage for one of his cars, something he's been doing since he learned to drive. Tracking a car's mileage is his way of monitoring an engine's performance. After each fill-up, he notes the number of gallons purchased and miles driven in a notebook he keeps in the cars. At the time he was sitting at the kitchen table, flipping through one of the notebooks. I was making dinner and could hear him mumbling, trying to recall the steps:

"Subtract the old odometer reading from the new one," he said. "Then what?"

He couldn't remember the next step, to divide the difference by the gallons purchased. Math had always been easy for Steve, but doing this simple equation is sometimes impossible now. When I offered to help, he pushed away from the table and said resignedly, "No. I'll do it when I'm able."

Sitting at the picnic table watching Elly arrange the flowers, I see Steve deep in thought, lost in the misery of his life. "I don't know who I'll be when this is over," he says.

Chapter 12

Rambler Rage

More than a year has passed since our overnight camping trip, and Steve's mental health continues to decline, even though he's taking his meds. People with mental illnesses don't always take the drugs they're prescribed. Some don't like the side effects; others think they don't need them. And there are people like Steve who need to be reminded every day. Lithium has evened his mood, and the antidepressant prevents the deep lows he once had. But he still ruminates about his thwarted campaign against SAE. And he continues to have mild hallucinations. These often occur at the onset of bipolar disorder but fade as the mind rebalances itself. Steve sometimes hears music that isn't there or sees the ceiling move above

the chair where he sits for hours each
day.

The psychiatrist Steve saw at the
time of his breakdown told me that people
with bipolar disorder often recover and go
on to lead full lives. Two-and-a-half years
have passed since Detroit, and Steve is
still significantly compromised. I continue
to lower my expectations about our future.

To help him manage his daily routine, I usually make a list so he can remember what he wants to do. Even with
a list, his days are challenging. If he has
errands to run before attending a parents'
ice hockey meeting in the evening, he'll jot
down the number of minutes he expects
each stop will take. Working backwards,
he'll figure out when he has to leave to get
everything done. I saved one of his calcu-
lations; it reads: "RC auto parts, 15; grocery, 30; wine, 15; Wal-Mart, 30; Sears,
30; walk, 75." Each stop is numbered in
the order he wants it to occur. After total-
ing the minutes, he subtracts them from
when the parent meeting begins. The note
continues: "Meeting 6:00 - 3.25 = 2:45 Lv."

Sometimes this approach works, other times it doesn't. He frequently drives past a scheduled stop and has to circle back. Or he goes to the wrong school to get Elly after soccer practice, which frustrates all of us: Steve, because he screwed up; Elly, because the soccer coach has to call me to come get her; and me, because I have to leave work early. Steve frequently shares his inability to successfully complete tasks with his psychiatrist. He told the doctor how it once took him three trips to the grocery to get three things. We live about fifteen minutes from the closest store, so he spent a good part of the afternoon driving back and forth to the store. The psychiatrist expressed concern, but also told Steve that his sharing this with him made "a perfect teaching moment" for the medical residents he oversees at the university. It'll help them understand how complicating a mental illness diagnosis can be, the doctor said.

Creating daily to-do lists for Steve took getting used to for both of us. They made me feel overbearing, but I also felt that they allowed him to be less responsible than he possibly could be. For Steve, having lists meant learning to accept his limitations as well as the constant input of another, even if it was from someone he loved. Initially, neither of us understood whether these mental deficits were symptoms of the disorder or the result of the medications. Either way, to-do lists seemed necessary, and eventually they became a regular part of our routine.

Steve also devised his own ways of getting around his short-term memory problems. If he wanted to tell the family something, he frequently left notes on the kitchen counter. A sampling: "Linda. Shouldn't we have heard back on my stress test?" "Elly, you left three long extension cords in the grass after your party, almost hit one with the mower." And, my favorite, "Linda, please don't unbutton the little buttons on my shirt collar when you wash them. Thanks, Steve."

For a while he wore a small tape recorder on his belt loop, and when at home a pint-size jug bottle around his neck if he wanted to remember to turn off a water spigot or remove a car battery from the charger. The children also learned to navigate around Steve's memory challenges. In a journal entry, I wrote how twelve-year-old Elly deftly managed one of Steve's lapses: "At dinner last night Elly was telling us something that happened at school when Steve blurted out, 'Oh! I've got to remember to tell you something.' He squeezed both sides of his head, as if trying to physically keep the thought from escaping. Elly, without missing a beat, turned to her father and said, 'Daddy, give me a word,' and he said, 'penguins.' With that, Steve relaxed and Elly went on to finish her story." I didn't record her story, but I did note that when she finished, Steve told us that friends had offered us two free tickets to an upcoming Pittsburgh Penguins hockey game.

Adjusting to this new normal didn't happen easily or quickly. It was especially difficult for Steve, who had to learn to live with his loss. When he was mentally stable, he willingly welcomed our help. When psychosis flared, though, as it did every couple of months, he ignored input from family.

• • •

It's a late September afternoon more than a year after the camping trip. I'm sitting in my office at the newspaper when the phone rings. It's John; he sometimes calls after school to check in.

"I think you should know that Pop is taking the Ramblers from behind the barn and pulling them up the driveway," says John, who naturally assumes a more watchful role when I'm not at home. This wasn't something we talked about; it just happened. John sounds matter of fact, as if he's telling me that Elly's soccer game has been canceled. But I can hear the underlying tension in his voice.

"He's got three at the top and is pulling another one through the yard," he says. "The brakes are seized, and it's tearing up the lawn."

Since moving to Pennsylvania, Steve has accumulated six broken-down Ramblers that he keeps behind the barn. Two were totaled in accidents; the others are parts cars he got for free or cheaply. He uses them to keep our two working

Ramblers running. I complain frequently about being able to see the cars from the living room window, and I want him to move them deeper into the pasture, out of sight.

In my mind, I link Steve's obsession with Ramblers to his faltering mental health. Like the SAE paraphernalia that once infiltrated our home, Rambler stuff is everywhere, from the cap he wears to the Rambler clock that's shaped like a hubcap, which replaced the John Deere clock on our living room wall. There are Rambler calendars and coffee cups and tee shirts. He even wraps the garden hose around an old Rambler wheel and decorated the exterior perimeter of the garage doors with two-dozen hubcaps (each equidistant from one another). I tolerate this obsession because I've learned to pick my fights, but I hate seeing the broken-down Ramblers by the barn. Steve's agreed to move them, but wants John and Luke to help.

It isn't easy moving 3,500-pound hunks of metal, especially when the wheels don't turn. And when he does move them, he wants them arranged neatly in the lower pasture. Using a length of bale twine to measure, he plans to position each of the front ends equidistant from the fencerow and spaced evenly apart. Whenever Steve tries getting the boys to help, they have a ready excuse, homework or hockey practice or something else. Whatever it is, they easily talk their way out of helping. Then he wants me to intervene. I resist.

"You have to take charge," I tell him. "They're teenagers. You have to make them do it."

"They won't," comes his childlike reply.

"Don't ask them. Tell them," I say. "You're the father. I hate to be the one to enforce your will."

Although I try distancing myself from situations like this, I usually end up in the middle. I understand why the kids don't want to help, because Steve is overly obsessive about all things Rambler. But I also feel the tug of my own upbringing, that a father's wishes should be respected. But where is the line between respect for a parent and what is reasonable to ask of a child? I struggle frequently to find a balance between the two. Despite my effort, Steve complains often about how I fail to support what he wants. Months have passed since we began bickering about moving the cars, but they're still there. But from what John is telling me on the phone, Steve has taken the matter into his own hands. He isn't dragging them deeper into the pasture, like we talked about, but pulling them through the yard and up our steep driveway.

I leave work immediately. By the time I get home, Steve is maneuvering the last Rambler into place. Pulling into the driveway, I see a pile of broken-down cars lining the front edge of our property and protruding onto the neighbor's. He's created an eyesore that will embarrass me into taking action. Later he told me: "I knew that if I could get your attention, you'd make them help." As kind as Steve can be when his mind is stable, he's equally as retaliatory when he's not well.

Pulling my car alongside the tractor, I call to him. "What are you doing?" I speak loud enough to be heard but don't want to sound angry. I can see the intensity with which he works. His face is determined, his focus solely on pushing the last car into place. He doesn't' answer my question.

Whenever Steve is manic, he avoids interacting with me. In the years following Detroit, we both eventually came to understand my role in helping him maintain balance in his life. We joke frequently about my being his "governor," a reference to the engine part that regulates speed. Steve usually doesn't mind my help. Multiple hospitalizations are common among people with severe mental illnesses, in part because when left to monitor their own actions, they often see them through a distorted lens. Steve's allowing me to help him was instrumental in preventing additional hospitalizations. But when his mind tips toward psychotic, he won't listen to anyone. He avoids eye contact with me, for he wants nothing to pull him from the mania that empowers him. When John told me on the phone that he tried talking to his father and he wouldn't listen, I knew the situation was serious.

After maneuvering the last Rambler into place, Steve drives the Fergie to the barn, leaving me to wonder what I'm supposed to do. Walking back up the hill from the barn, he passes me in the driveway but doesn't stop. Then, without looking back, he yells, "Tell John and Luke they won't see my face until those cars are lined up the way I want them." With that he retreats downstairs to the home office and locks the door.

"Your father isn't well," I say to Luke and Elly with more authority than I feel. They're home from school now and are rummaging through the pantry for an after-school snack. "He's resting in the office. You're on your own until I figure out what to do."

"Why are the cars up there?" Elly wants to know. She's in the third grade and Luke the eighth. Neither will like their friends seeing a lineup of broken-down cars when getting off and on the school bus. John, a senior, drives to school.

"I don't know," I say. "I need you to be helpful and start your homework. I'm going to make a few phone calls. Then maybe John and I will get the cars down. I just don't know yet."

There is no guidebook on how to respond when someone is experiencing a psychotic incident. With repeated occurrences, patterns emerge, yet each event feels unique and wrought with uncertainty. Are we to drag the cars back down the hill? Or will that provoke him further? Will he leave to wander the country roads if we do? Or will he leave if we don't? What about the children? How embarrassing is it to wait for the school bus by a pile of rusting Ramblers?

Luke says nothing, holding himself tight against an urge to lash out at his father. He's learning how to react, although I know his anger will surface after the crisis passes. He will argue as he has before that his father could control himself if he wanted to. He also will blame me for not standing up to Steve. I allow Luke these rants, for Nancy listens to mine. It's the least I can do for a child who has endured so much. In the three years since his accident, Luke has adapted well to seeing

through a single lens, but he's self-con-
scious about his misshapen eye. The iris
is deformed and the eye often red. Years
later, when he's in college and I have better health insurance, a prosthesis similar
in color and shape to his good eye will be
fitted over the damaged one.

Nancy is still at work, so I call a
neighbor whose own husband was diagnosed as bipolar early in their marriage.
She and her husband are divorced, but
she is one who understands the challenges I face. The two of us attended the
twelve-week NAMI education course last
year, and the two of us talk frequently.
Her house is across the road and, like
ours, built part way down a steep hill.

When she answers, I say, "Take a
look out your window. Steve's not doing
well, and I'm not sure what to do."

When I describe what's happened,
her first question is whether Steve will
harm himself.

"I don't think so," I say. "He's locked
himself in the office; he'll probably stay
there all night."

"What about you and the kids?" she

asks. Trained as a nurse, she knows the importance of first assessing everyone's safety. Talking to her helps me decide what to do.

"No," I say, feeling more assured, "we're okay." We are three years in to this kind of behavior, and I feel more confident with each occurrence.

Although I worry about Steve taking his own life, he's never physically threatened the children or me. I've sat through several medical appointments when he's told the doctor that he thinks about hurting himself. We still have Grandpa Schmitmeyer's old shotgun and rifle in our home. They are locked in a gun safe, and I have the key. I think about getting rid of them but intuitively know that if Steve ever tried taking his own life, it would involve an automobile. It's an odd thing to know about your husband, but I do. A notion firmly imbedded in my understanding of him.

"I don't think it's necessary to involve the police," I tell my neighbor. "But I'm going to try reaching his doctor."

It's after five o'clock when I call, so

I'm connected to a nurse, who tells me what I already know: to get Steve to an emergency room and, if I feel threatened in any way, to call the police. I know I can't call the police, for one thing is clear since Detroit. Steve will never be taken against his will again.

"Let's go, John," I say when I hang up the phone. "We're going to get the cars down."

Enough time has passed for me to know that I'm not acting impulsively or out of anger. More so, I'm following my gut—that it's okay to bring them down from the road. I also remember that Steve said the boys would not see his face until the cars were where he wanted them to be.

"But it's raining," worries Elly.

"It's only a drizzle. It'll make it easier getting them down," I say, trying to add levity to the situation. At times like this, a feeling of certainty often surfaces in me, a way of reassuring the children that everything will be okay.

"Let's get them to the bottom of the driveway tonight," I say to John. "We can

figure out how to get them down to the
pasture tomorrow."

"Is Pop okay with that?" John asks.

"He said he wants you boys to get
them down," I say. "We need to get going;
it'll be dark soon."

As John and I drag the last Rambler to the bottom of the driveway, I see
movement in the back yard. It is Steve
under the cover of the darkening sky
moving stealthily toward the barn. Why
is he watching us? Is he angry at what
we're doing? Maybe he's planning to leave
again?

I go to the barn and call his name,
but he doesn't answer. He's hiding somewhere inside, but I know not to look for
him. Later, when his mind is less volatile,
he tells me that he was in the haymow. He
also said that he heard me on the phone;
he was worried that the police might come
to get him: "If they came," he said, "I
planned to jump headfirst from the barn
roof." I shudder. There are no guidelines
on how to deal with a psychotic episode.
Only intuition. And the accumulated understanding garnered from previous inci-

dents.

Later in the evening, I am in the kitchen packing lunches. I know Steve has returned to his office, because I heard the thud of the basement door. He will stay there all night, except when he hears Elly in the bathroom brushing her teeth as she gets ready for bed. Quietly he ascends the steps, and when she looks up, he's there, framed in the mirror, smiling down at her.

"I don't want you to worry," he says, bending to touch her back. "I'm really okay." He even teases her about how wild he'd been earlier in the evening. Then, as quickly and quietly as he came, he's back downstairs.

Elly carries a vivid memory of that exchange with her father. Watching the drama unfold outside our house through a bedroom window, she also saw Steve hiding behind the barn, watching John and me tow the cars down the driveway. That image contrasted sharply with the smiling, caring father who an hour later stood at the bathroom door. These conflicting impressions lay beyond the understanding of an eight-year-old. Years later, during a high school art class, she will explore what happened that night in a painting titled "Chutes and Lithium." The drawing is of a child's board game in which a pill-lined path winds between a house and barn, beside which stands the silhouetted figure of a man peering towards the house. Another one of her high school art projects, titled "Bipolar," is of three sculptured brains, each on a wooden pedestal of varying heights and connected to one another by a rusty wire. The brains depict the highs and lows of bipolarity: The first brain is smooth and intact; the second, cracked and broken; and the third, with pills scattered around its base, whole but misshapen by deep fissures. The sculpture won first place in the county's high school arts festival.

Although gentle towards Elly, Steve is less forgiving of John and Luke. The next morning, in keeping with his promise that they wouldn't be allowed to see him until the cars have been properly lined up in the pasture, he comes into the kitchen with a bathrobe draped over his head. A myriad of emotions surface when I see him: anger, sadness, self-pity. "This is my husband," I think. "This is my life." Like Luke, my anger emerges when fear fades.

As Steve's mind stabilizes over the next several days, he slowly reintegrates himself into our family, even joking with the boys about "wildly pulling the cars up the driveway." On the following Saturday, when he asks them to help him move the cars deeper into the pasture, they willingly agree. Again, they push and pull the cars with the Fergie. It takes several hours, and when they return to the house, they are subdued. Complying with Steve's whims is difficult, I know, but they say little. Only later, when family life returns to normal, do they tease their father about how obsessive he was in arranging the cars in the pasture.

As for the Ramblers, they will stay there for another seven years, out of eyeshot from the living room windows, but not necessarily off my mind.

Chapter 13

Through Steve's Eyes: Data Points

Steve and I struggled for years to truly understand how mental illness affects personality, how being diagnosed with mental illness at times made him act and think differently than he otherwise did. It begs the question of who we really are and of whether we are merely the aggregation of our thoughts and behaviors. How much control do we have over our personalities? I often thought about what role Steve's seemingly idyllic earlier life played in helping him regain a semblance of the person he once was. It takes immense willpower to emerge from a mental illness, and Steve's inherent understanding of who he was before he got sick seemed critical in being able to recover. For many years Steve had been a thoughtful man. A good father. A caring husband. A talented engineer. His illness changed that.

Even though our life continued to appear as it had been—we lived in the same house (thanks to financial help from Steve's parents) and did many of the same things we'd done before—Steve's and my relationship felt very different because Steve *was* different. Not always, but sometimes. It showed up in characteristics that hadn't been there before. In his anger and thoughtlessness. His impulsivity and self-absorption. His abandoning care for his family. Still I stayed with a man who at times was so different from who he'd been, for despite these changes, he never stopped trying to get better.

He continued to make regular visits to his therapist and psychiatrist. And he participated in a half-dozen clinical trials at the Stanley Center. In one psychotherapy trial, investigators closely monitored participants' daily interpersonal and social routines in an effort to determine their effect on mood swings. This required extensive input from Steve as the re-

searchers worked to understand the ever-
shifting nature of his illness. To that end,
Steve made weekly visits to Pittsburgh
and tracked for several months his daily
activities as well as his mood. He wrote
down everything from when he woke up
to when he got out of bed. From his first
meal to his initial interaction with another. From getting dressed in the morning
to going outdoors. And so on... It took a
great deal of time and energy for someone
who at times had trouble getting out of
bed in the morning.

While the psychotherapy trial didn't
result in any significant change in Steve's
treatment protocol, it did reinforce my
willingness to remain with him, especially
in light of what one of the co-investigators
said the year after Steve began taking
an antipsychotic drug again. One of the
Stanley Center's initiatives was to edu-
cate the public about symptoms of mental
illness. They also wanted to enlist people
with bipolar disorder to become part of
the center's patient registry. A local television reporter interviewed one of the co-investigators for the station's evening news

segment, and he asked the co-investigator to identify someone who may have bipolar disorder. She answered, "What you often see in a person with bipolar disorder is someone who looks like he doesn't care about his family."

That's how it often felt, that Steve cared only for himself. And that's why divorce statistics for marriages involving a person with bipolar disorder are especially high, ninety percent, according to a 2003 article, "Managing Bipolar Disorder," in *Psychology Today*.

During these very difficult years, Steve's and my energies were turned inward, away from casual friends and extraneous activities. I focused on giving our children the stable life I thought so important, in which kids had sleepovers and ice skating parties while moms and dads went to the theater or played cards with friends on Saturday evenings. I was mostly alone in my effort to maintain our family life, for Steve was consumed with his own challenge—healing a mind plagued by fluctuating moods and unquiet thoughts. Those who were aware of what

our life was like empathized with me, for
they identified with the challenges I faced.

But few can imagine Steve's struggle. In his mid-forties, he had to find a
new way of moving forward with a mind
different from what it had been. A mind
he could no longer trust to perceive things
as others did. He also had to come to
terms with the humiliation of knowing
that what he thought was a noble effort—
to help an engineering society regain its
footing—was viewed as insanity by others. Understanding this, he had to find a
way to put to rest the demons set loose by
his crusade. His struggle was horrific, an
internal battle he faced alone; and for the
most part, without the empathy of others,
for few of us really understand that kind
of challenge. Still, he persevered.

• • •

"I plan to leave work early to get
Elly from soccer practice," I say to Steve,
who is sitting at the kitchen table eating
a bowl of Cheerios. It's been two months
since he pulled the Ramblers to the top of

the hill. He has a psychiatrist's appointment in Pittsburgh this afternoon, and I'm
headed to work. He sees the doctor every
week now because he's participating in
a new trial. The doctor has recently reintroduced an antipsychotic medication,
Risperdal, similar to the drug he took for
six months following his hospitalization.

"I can get her," he offers.

"You can't," I say. "It's Thursday.
You have a Stanley Center appointment."

"Oh yeah," he says. "What time?"

"Three. I marked it down. You'll
want to leave early to get gas. I printed
out my notes for the doctor," I say, mo-
tioning to the paper on the island counter.
At the top I'd written, "Linda's observations since Steve's last visit."

Following his breakdown, Steve
switched psychiatrists several times in
an effort to find one who might help him
get better. He eventually ended up at the
Stanley Center, which at the time was
associated with the University of Pittsburgh. The psychiatrists there were more
aggressive in their treatment, which Steve
and I liked. His doctor might prescribe a

medication or supplement, and instead of waiting several months to monitor its effectiveness, as his previous doctors had done, he would increase or decrease the dosage in a matter of weeks. Or he might add a different one. Because he's on a new medication and I'm unable to join him for this appointment, I write down what I have observed during the past week.

Steve picks up the paper and reads:

• On Friday, Steve's mood dropped somewhat. He was irritable and angry. He was less able to focus on a conversation or the task at hand.

• This irritability did not last throughout the week. After a day, his mood elevated even though his ability to function did not.

• Pacing the floor has increased significantly. He walks around in a daze, no direction; unable to follow through and complete tasks. When we talk, he has to concentrate to understand what I'm saying.

• On Saturday, changing a battery in one of the smoke detectors seemed too difficult and stressful.

• Sleep has decreased and it is often interrupted. He no longer takes a nap. After 3-4 hours, he is up, unable to sleep. Several nights he fell back to sleep in a recliner while watching TV. He probably gets between 5 and 7 hours, total. This is down from his usual 9-plus hours.

• He eats a lot more; 'It's something to do,' he says.

• His body is very rigid, and he's uncomfortable while sitting and sleeping. At times, his mouth hangs slightly open.

• In the past 36 hours, the symptoms seem to be improving somewhat. On Tuesday, he slept in bed for 7 hours straight. After being sidetracked during our lunch conversation on Wednesday, he returned to a point he wanted to make. He couldn't

even follow a conversation
earlier in the week.

• Although he has functioned
at a very low level this week,
he does not seem particularly
depressed.

Rifling through the kitchen catch-all
drawer, Steve grabs a pencil and adds:

• Anxiety especially when falling asleep at night.

• Avoid public functions—Did
not go to the hockey club
board meeting last night (I'm
vice chairman). Also may
not go to Linda's work Xmas
party this Sat. night.

In the most acute stages of Steve's
illness the two of us spent a great deal of
time assessing his symptoms. For Steve to
do this alone was impossible because he
lives largely in the moment, answering the
doctor's questions about how he's been
feeling throughout the week by telling him
how he feels at that moment. This is partially because he has poor recall, but also
because of who he is. Astute in analyzing

technical problems, he was never inclined to reflect on his own thoughts, feelings, and actions.

Steve's psychiatric appointments always begin with a therapist or the doctor asking about his behaviors since his last visit, his alcohol consumption, sleep habits, fluctuations in mood, thoughts of hurting himself or others, and so on. These questions are standard and designed to reveal shifts in mood and thinking since the previous visit.

To aid his recall, Steve began tracking his thoughts and noting observations about his behaviors in notebooks and on loose-leaf paper. Data points, he called his writing, bulleted bits of information, some of which he shared with his doctor and therapist. After one appointment with his therapist, he wrote:

> Going to my Oct. 3 appt. was not normal. Left with time to get gas, passed the therapist's office and made a U-turn. Then realized I had time to get gas and made another U-turn to get gas. Returned to his office and found of-

fice door locked. I was supposed to meet him at his
other office. Also I would have
forgotten the appt. if Linda
hadn't reminded me. When I
had to pick up Elly after the
missed appointment, I drove
to the wrong school. Couldn't
remember that she had
changed schools, but that
was two months ago.

The therapist was bewildered by
Steve's lack of improvement. At his next
appointment, he told Steve that within a
year of a major episode people who are
compliant with taking medication should
be 75 to 80 percent back to normal.

Steve frequently jotted down information in preparation for his visits to the
psychiatrist and the therapist. In the following, written in preparation for a doctor
visit two years after Detroit, he wrote:

Main Problem: Broken mind,
cannot think clearly or mo-
tivate my body to do something. Not even hobbies. That
sucks. Problem with reading
and long division.

Drawing a box around the words, he went on to analyze his Main Problem in hopes of finding a solution. The data points continued:

> • Li (lithium) and Wellbutrin (antidepressant) have not helped my Main Problem.
> • Would one of them be contributing to my Main Problem?
> • Could read electrical drawings when on Haldol, but not now.
> • I'm gradually getting worse with thinking; reading and math are more difficult with time.

Steve periodically kept notes about his illness for several years. The data points mostly centered around visits to his therapist, who helped him understand the multitude of changes that can occur with a mental disorder. The data points began several months before he left for Detroit and continued while his mind was unstable, until a psychiatrist reintroduced an antipsychotic almost three years after Detroit. Then the doctor prescribed

Risperdal instead of Haldol, because it has fewer side effects. When Steve began taking Risperdal his mind became clearer, not as it had once been, but far better than without the medication. He could again follow conversations and calculate the gas mileage of his cars, and, most importantly, those potentially dangerous episodes—like pulling Ramblers to the top of the driveway—stopped.

Steve wrote his notes in the typical, data-gathering style he once used to solve engineering problems, short phrases preceded by a small, black pencil dot. His writings were an eye-opener when I first read them several years after they were written, because they revealed the depth of his struggle. They also helped me see again the engaged, analytical, and, at times, witty man I married—not the apathetic and uncaring man he often appeared to be.

What follows are excerpts of Steve's writings, which tell of his struggle far better than I am able. (The parentheses are mine.)

Feb. 7, 1995 (written shortly before leaving for Detroit)
• Making a positive impact on SAE for my 25 years of dedicated membership. If this cannot be done, I'm in real trouble, because it is the only thing that needs to be done for me to want to contribute to society again in a way that I am naturally inclined/driven...

Sept. 13, 1995 (several months after Detroit)
• All hinges on me being able to work again, male thing.
• My head is not with me.
• Need to see work progress to enjoy anything again. Otherwise, slipping back to bipolar or other non-productive state of mind seems possible, and it almost seems restful just to stay there.

Oct. 9, 1995
• Don't feel right making follow up calls (with Plasquip customers), need to get in right mood.
• SAE = feeling frustrated, angry, mad.
• Psychiatrist says, "Drop it."

Oct. 12, 1995
• I don't like myself.
• Cannot enjoy nice weather. Cannot enjoy hobbies, Ramblers, etc.
• I'm no longer a provider.
• Linda says I was talking in my sleep. I said, I'll tell you what the problem is. I'm scared to death. That's the problem. I'm scared to death.

Oct. 24, 1995 (after participating in an Occupational Vocation Rehabilitation seminar)
• I have my own values and can take them with me in whatever job I do.
• Need to grieve; SAE was important part of my life.
• Told my therapist that my values may be good, but if corporate America doesn't operate on these values, what good are they to take with me in whatever job I end up doing.

Oct. 30, 1995
• Linda's frustration, anger, and fear is building by my not working.
• Talked with therapist about why I moved SAE box back

into my office/he didn't like
it.
• Linda would like me to burn
the SAE box.
• Her support is a Must or I
will crumble.
• Linda wants me to set specific criteria and deadline for
reaching goals if I'm to continue with Plasquip. Says that
I don't have to give my loyalty
to another company, just my
time. Says I'm not the only
one who got screwed.

Nov. 20, 1995
• Not able to work Monday
afternoon or all day Tuesday.
Rotten feeling.
• Realizing I may not be able
to work again, a sinking
truth.
• Pain in my chest/hurt. Unsure of future.
• Linda won't have a husband
that does nothing.
• Inability to get an answer
from Jack still haunts me.
• Therapist said I should be
stabilized from the drugs by
this time. He said my desire
not to work is part of my illness, and that I should con-
sider part-time work: Burger
King? IKEA?

November 1995
• Applied for a part-time
job to assemble furniture at
IKEA; spent an hour in parking lot working up courage to
go inside. Can I work being so
afraid?

• • •

Steve's lack of confidence in applying for the IKEA job contrasts sharply to
the confidence he felt when starting work
as a staff engineer at SAE. The kids and
I were still living in Ohio then, and he
called home at the end of his first day to
tell me how it went. He was in Langley,
Virginia, at a NASA research center, not
at SAE's headquarters in Pennsylvania,
where I thought he would be.

"Virginia?" I asked. "What are you
doing there?"

"I got a brief orientation; then they
sent me to Langley for a committee meeting," he said.

Steve's boss wanted him there
as SAE's representative during a landing gear committee meeting being held

at Langley. The Challenger space shuttle
had exploded earlier that year, and all
aspects of its construction were under
scrutiny. NASA got more involved in the
landing gear committee's work and was
hosting the bi-annual committee meeting.
Although Steve had traveled to dozens of
U.S. air force bases in his fourteen years
as an engineer for Wright-Patterson, this
was his first trip to a NASA facility, and
he was excited.

"Wasn't that hard?" I asked. The
idea of having to speak before a technical
committee on the first day of any new job
would have been my undoing. Steve was
undaunted, confident in his dealing with
the exchange of technical information.

"No. No," he said. "They told me
what to say. It was easy."

Nine years later, when applying for
a part-time job at IKEA, it took an hour
for him to muster courage to go inside
and fill out an application. On Dec. 3,
1995, he received a letter from IKEA:
"Dear Mr. Schmitmeyer: Thank you for
taking the time to complete an application
for employment at IKEA Pittsburgh. Cur-

rently, we do not have a position..." The next day, he wrote in his notebook:

Dec. 4, 1995
• Overcome by strong SAE feelings. Don't feel good that I had to stop midstream. Everyone tells me to stop, forget it, think of something else, drop it, ignore it, etc. No one is willing to help me bring it to an end. I think I'll just keep chipping away at SAE when I meet friends and SAE staff at the Pittsburgh chapter meetings.
• Being a 25-year member and staff engineer at SAE, I know and have seen things. It's like being involved in our govt. and seeing minor corruption being allowed in your area, and you have the ability to bring it to people's attention and have it dealt with. But in my case, I'm being told to just stop and let the corruption go on in my own society.
• Why does SAE stop me from working while others can leave and work at other jobs?

Dec. 11, 1995

• Therapist talked about possibly getting closure by taking two weekends to write a letter that I would send to SAE's Board of Directors.

• He wrote a lot when I talked about SAE. Made me nervous. I hope I'm not going to be re-admitted or given shock treatment against my will. I just don't trust the systems; he could be giving info to SAE/FBI, who knows. But I'm still willing to write (those letters) if Linda doesn't leave me. If I do, I think I could work Plasquip better or look for a job better. Also SAE wouldn't invade my mind when I'm raking leaves, driving the car or trying to sleep.

• I went through my SAE box and put my complaints on sheets of paper. I don't think I'll send these because Linda won't put up with it.

Dec. 19, 1995

• Just finished OVR's (Occupational Vocational Rehabilitation) 1-day testing, and I don't like who I'm becoming as a result of the SAE Incident in Detroit. It's made

me less trusting, less confident, more introverted. I miss
weeks of my life and am more
likely to go down the social
ladder than up. Jobs that
have some appeal are police-
man for a local township or
a union rep that would bring
workers' views to manage-
ment.

Dec. 20, 1995

• Linda and I had a big argument before I got out of bed.
It revolves around me not
working and ends with cold
tea thrown in my face.

• • •

The cold-tea fight was about what
we always fight about, his lack of support
for the family.

"How can you lay there when you
know how much I need your help?" I ask.
My voice is strained, high-pitched. The
children have left for school, so my wrath
is unguarded. I'm leaving for work, and
Steve is still in bed. I begin again. "When I
come home tonight I have to make dinner
and fix a treat for Elly's Christmas party.

Presents need wrapping, and I still don't have anything for your parents. If you can't work at Plasquip, the least you can do is help around here. You can't expect me to do everything."

Steve is in his favorite sleeping position, on his stomach with his right arm above his head, his left arm by his side. He faces the edge of the bed. When I talk, he turns his head away. His arms automatically adjust to the new position.

Enraged, I try a new tactic, one I'm sure will make him pay attention.

"It's SAE!" I yell. "That goddam box again."

Two months ago Steve took the box of SAE correspondence from our closet where he'd kept it since his hospitalization. The psychiatrist told him not to open it, and his therapist said he should burn it. Now he has it in his office and probably spends his days rereading the letters he wrote.

Steve had taken the box with him to Detroit, but it was left at his cousin's house when he was transferred to St. Rita's. He fretted about getting it back

throughout the three-hour drive to Lima,
so his cousin brought it to him while he
was still in the hospital. Since then he's
carefully guarded its whereabouts. He's
hit a new low since he put it in his office;
now he's unable or unwilling to work at
Plasquip or anything else. Christmas is
five days away, and he won't get out of
bed.

"I can't take much more of this," I
say, and I see his body tense at my words.
Intuitively, I know Steve is afraid I might
leave him, and sometimes I play on that
fear. Slowly, as if the motion itself is painful, he turns back toward me. Raising
himself on an elbow, he stares blankly at
me. He's technically complying with my
wish for his attention, yet says nothing.
I'm already late for work, and he hasn't
offered to help. Anger surges within, and I
toss a half-empty mug of cold tea into his
face. Then I walk out the door.

January 1996
• A good month workwise.

March 4, 1996
• In Church I realized I was
'raped' by SAE in Detroit, af-

ter being misled for 25 years.
I felt as if I had been taken
against my will, stripped,
forced/restrained to a bed,
injected—to put me out 'til
the next day, no phone call
home. I'm trying to get back.
I really lack trust in organizations. Also my self-confidence
is gone.

March 6, 1996
• I wish I could stay home
and do nothing, or return to
the hospital. I don't think the
hospital would cure me; it
would just be a place to exist.
• I still think that some communication with SAE would
help me. It could be verbal.
• If I cannot work, I may lose
my wife and kids and house.
Our savings and retirement
money are gone. Need help
before I lose what's most important to me.
• I'm not sure what kind of a
worker/person I am.
• If I apply for a job, do I tell
an employer I'm bipolar?

March 7, 1996
• Dr. appt.
• Mood swings milder and
shorter than some days.

• No hallucinations, alcohol abuse, spending sprees.

March 22, 1996
• Trying to improve the system is almost a religion to me, but the System has knocked me down: gun search, handcuffs, strapped to bed, knocked out with shot, FBI, Pinkerton following me, idea of me killing Jack, armed guard for Jack.
• Not productive at Plasquip.

July 17, 1996
• Last three months have been working fairly good, although sales haven't been that great.
• Question my worth and my ability to work in the future.
• Afraid that someday I may want to be a vegetable rather than support my family.
• I often get down/unproductive periods after a big weekend or event, like having someone visit us. I cannot work but can sleep day and night.

Throughout his illness, Steve somehow managed to function fairly well when other people were around. If we went away for a weekend, he had sufficient stamina to interact for extended periods of time with friends or family. But when we returned home, he often sunk into a deep depression and slept or did nothing for days. I was terribly frustrated by this for a long time, believing that if he was capable of doing things and controlling his mood around others, he could do so at home. I'd accuse him of not trying hard enough for his family.

Eventually I understood that Steve was doing what others with physical illnesses often do, keep their symptoms in check when called upon to do so. I likened it to my going to work when not feeling well and working productively throughout the day, only to collapse when I got home. With time I realized that the increased stimuli of these social interactions stressed Steve's fragile mind, and he recovered best by being quiet. It's why he slept so much when we returned home or sat in his chair for hours on end. It was a tough lesson to learn and a difficult aspect of his illness to accept. It also felt isolating, because others would never really know the depth of my frustration nor the complexity of living with someone who has a mental illness.

July 25, 1996
• Not sure I want to go into a job hiding the fact that I'm Bipolar.
• It would be nice if there was a way I could help support my family in a job I like, with a non-corrupt employer I respected.

Aug. 15, 1996
• Got lost at a Bridgeville (Pa.) intersection and was so anxious that I could hardly speak to get directions.
• Sometimes my self-confidence is so low I'm not able to discipline my kids.
• I feel like my usefulness is slipping away.
• It's nice to be home to help John, Luke, and Elly, but when I do, I immediately pull away, feeling bad that I cannot help myself to help our family more. I know it is important and I know I'll be left with little to live for if they leave me.

• The stress of my minimal contributions leaves me with a pain in my breastbone and a queasy stomach.

Dec. 23 1996
• I woke up at 3:15 a.m. with suicide on my mind. I came up with what felt like a perfect way to send a strong message to SAE. It wouldn't hurt anyone except the feelings of my family and others who are close to me. I can leave all my identification behind and take a bus into Pittsburgh. I could throw myself under a dual-wheeled truck as it rounds the corner.

March 10, 1997
•I exist. All I do is take in food and put out shit.

April 22, 1997
• I am only existing. I'm not able to think, read, work, and play with my kids.
• I wish my kids could ask me things without the how does Pop feel sound in their voice and look in their eyes.
• I have much less desire to "have the state take care of me." Being a street/home-

less person seems better than this.

Steve often talked about wanting to be homeless, to live on the streets free of responsibility. Seeing a panhandler in Pittsburgh or a beggar's bedroll stowed beneath one of the city's many bridges, he talked about the simplicity of their lives, of their freedom to do as they pleased. Steve never left to live on the streets, but his desire to escape his own life pulled strongly on him. It occasionally caused him to leave home without telling anyone he was going. His departures were always sudden and unannounced, for they occurred when mania flared and he wanted to be far away before anyone knew he was gone. I called them "episodes." They were by far the most terrifying aspect of his illness because they happened when his mind was unstable and his judgment impaired.

Chapter 14

Road Trip

"Where's your dad?" I say to John as he heaves an ice hockey bag into the trunk of his '68 Rambler American. We bought the light blue car for him shortly after he turned sixteen. It's similar to Steve's '65 Rambler, which Steve says allows for more uniform maintenance of our cars. Once enthusiastic about creating standards for the aerospace industry, Steve now looks for ways to systematize our home life. His handiwork is everywhere, in the multiple rows of wrenches hanging on the garage wall—from smallest to largest with heads facing the same way—to the cereal boxes in the pantry. Buying John's car was part of his push for an all-Rambler fleet. Despite his urgings, I still drive a *normal* car, my full-size

Pontiac station wagon.

Steve wanted John to have his own car even though I argued that we couldn't afford it. It will make him more responsible, said Steve, who loved the cherry red '63 Chevy convertible he drove in high school. I suspect John is less fond of his old-man sedan; it's decades older than what his friends drive. To personalize the Rambler, he installed a Jensen radio and 6-by-9 speakers on the parcel shelf behind the back seat.

Today John is headed for an afternoon ice hockey game. He slams the trunk and says, "He wasn't in his chair when I came upstairs."

It's a Sunday in mid-March, and John will be graduating from high school soon. I just got home from picking up Elly at religion class, and Steve's Rambler isn't in the driveway. Although Steve and I grew up in strict Catholic families and married in the church, we hadn't practiced our religion with any regularity for many years. That changed after Detroit.

"I think I'd like to start going to Mass again," Steve told me when he was

in St. Rita's. We were walking in an en-
closed garden behind the hospital, and
I was telling him about our week. He
walked stiffly beside me, and even though
little of what I said seemed to register,
I chattered on about John's upcoming
hockey banquet and a party for Elly's
sixth birthday. Then, without any segue
from what I was saying, Steve blurted
that he wanted to start going to church
again. I asked why, but he didn't have an
answer. I suspect the religious underpin-
nings from childhood may have felt like
the only stable thing in his life at the time.

Several months later we joined the
local parish. All five of us usually go to
nine o'clock Mass. Afterwards, Elly has
CCD classes, the church's religious in-
struction for children. Instead of waiting
for her, we drive home, and either Steve or
I pick her up an hour later.

I start breakfast when we get home.
The family meal is still important to me,
and we have just enough time to eat together when Elly gets home and before
John leaves. I'm making coffee cake, my
dad's recipe from his days at the bakery.

As I put the cake into the oven, the phone rings. It's my sister-in-law, Mary Ann. The two of us have gotten closer since she stayed with John and Luke while I was in Detroit. She married my brother, Bob, and our families get together occasionally for weekend visits. Their family is also part of the group that vacations at Rice Lake.

"Hey, I'm coming to Pittsburgh next week for a seminar," Mary Ann says. "Are you free for dinner some night?"

A hydrogeologist who works on coal-mine reclamation for the state of Ohio, Mary Ann has regional meetings in Pittsburgh several times a year. When she's in town she invites me for dinner or an overnight stay at her hotel. Sometimes Steve joins us for dinner, but I prefer it be just Mary Ann and I. While I'm reluctant to unload our family drama with just anyone, time alone with Mary Ann is a chance for me to talk openly about my unhappy life.

When I hang up I tell Steve of our dinner plans, teasingly saying that it's "for women only." I try to sound playful, like Mary Ann and I are planning a night on the town. I can hear that my voice is harsher than I want it to be, but that's how it is sometimes. I'm good at going through the motions of being a supportive wife for a man with a mental illness, but I'm not always good at masking my unhappiness. I know Steve is stung by what I said, but I don't apologize. Instead I change the subject.

"CCD's almost over. Should I get Elly, or do you want to?"

Not looking up, he shakes his head no.

I say nothing to ease the tension, although I know I should. Steve is no longer confident enough to engage in the normal give-and-take of a healthy relationship. I'm conscientious about not letting our differences escalate to outright arguments, for I fear the spike of his suppressed emotions. But there are times when I'm too worn down to care. This is one of those times. I leave to get Elly, and when I return fifteen minutes later, his car is gone.

"I don't know where he is," John says. "He seemed all right when I went to

get my hockey bag." The implications of
John's answer registers with both of us,
and we exchange glances. Could this be
another episode?

Steve began having episodes about
six months before Detroit, psychotic
breaks that cause him to act rashly, like
pulling Ramblers to the top of the hill, or,
more frequently, leaving home without
telling anyone where he's going. He'll drive
the back roads of western Pennsylvania
for hours, sometimes even a day or two.
His paranoia flares during an episode,
and Steve imagines people are following
him. While on the road he eats only at
restaurants with drive-through windows,
telling me that he always faces the road
so he can see if someone is coming to get
him. I don't worry about his hurting other
people when he's away; I'm afraid he'll
take his own life. He has a deep-seated
fear of being taken against his will, and if
a cop pulls him over for any reason, anything could happen.

"If someone tried stopping me, I'd
drive my car into a bridge abutment," he
said once.

Time slows to a trickle when Steve is away. Moments feel like minutes, minutes become hours. I spend most of the day at the island counter where I can see the driveway through my kitchen window. It's also where I keep busy making meals for the upcoming week. I try hiding my concern from the children. Luke spends a lot of time in his bedroom. His anger will surface when his father is safely home. Elly, a week shy of her eighth birthday, sits coloring at a small table in the corner of the kitchen. Digging through her big box of crayons, she finds one she likes and moves it rhythmically across the page, making a "pretty picture" to hang on the wall behind her desk. In my journal that night I write, "Elly is worried, hugs me and hates to leave my side."

As the hours pass, I slip more into the moment. I am peeling and chopping vegetables. Potatoes. Celery. Onions. I'm making potato soup, my mother's recipe. The vegetables simmer in a pool of hot milk and butter. Her special ingredient is *rivula*. Flour and egg kneaded with the thumb and forefinger into doughy lumps and dropped into scalded milk. Everyone likes these gooey chunks, especially Steve. Like Elly's coloring, I make soup to pass the time. Soup therapy, I tell Nancy when we talk.

The phone rings, pulling me back to where I am. It's John calling from a pay-phone at the ice rink. "Have we located everyone yet?" he asks. Is he trying to be light-hearted, I wonder, or masking his concern in front of friends? I tell him no, but that we are okay. That evening in my journal I write, "John knows I want him to go on with his own life and not be encumbered by all that is here." I also wonder if he talks to his best friend about Steve's illness. John and his friend have been close since the first grade, and his friend's parents are familiar with the complexity of a mental illness diagnosis. A family member—the friend's grandfather—was diagnosed late in life with bipolar disorder. Our children rarely have friends to our house, but John spends a lot of time at his friend's house. They have a backyard pool, and I like seeing John horsing around in it with his high school buddies.

`8

624

Their family is especially thoughtful to include John in whatever they do. They've taken him on weeklong camping trips and sailing with friends on the Chesapeake. Steve's sister, Joyce, does the same with Elly and Luke. In the summer they spend a week at their horse farm in Ohio. Free for a while from the tension in our home.

I call Nancy. After a few moments, we hang up, and she calls me back. Whenever I want to talk, Nancy picks up the tab, even on Five-Cent Sundays, like today. A nickel a minute means we can talk for an hour for only three bucks. We talk several times a week, and our conversations often last long. She says her husband never complains about the phone bill. Talking to her is my lifeline; I couldn't do this without her. Today we talk several times. Mostly about whether my comment about dinner alone with Mary Ann triggered the episode. In retrospect, it becomes clearer, but at the time my understanding is vague. It could have been one of several things we talked about while I was fixing breakfast. I really didn't mean anything by my remark; I just need to be

free of this place every once in a while.
Nancy and I wonder about the effect of
Steve's episodes on the children. We talk
about that a lot, and she frequently tells
me they will be okay. "Kids are resilient,"
she says. "They're going to be fine."

The hours tick away. My fear spikes
as time passes. So does my anger. Another phone call to Nancy. My life is like
walking on eggshells, I say. I'm losing
hope and don't know how much more of
these ups and downs I can take. It's been
a horrendous year. Towing the Ramblers
uphill. The seat belts. And this.

My mind wanders to the evening
when Steve was washing the seat belts.
It seemed to be a turning point, where I
just couldn't keep going. I left that night
because I couldn't face the craziness; I felt
like I was going to explode.

I remember slamming the door
when I left, shutting myself off from
John's penetrating gaze. Silently I crossed
the cement pad. Spurred by the cool
night air and my longing to be free. Up
the steep driveway I ran. To nowhere.
Only *away* from here. From the turmoil

inside. Pivoting on the gravel, I turned downhill towards the barn. I stumbled, and the gravel cut my hand. The pain felt good. Distracting. Real. Something I understood. Then I swung wide around the dogwood tree outside Luke's bedroom window. I knew he was in there; instinctively I hunched to avoid being seen. I cried. Great sobs mingling with heaving breaths. Crazed and without direction. Down towards the barn. Back up to the gentle slope behind our home. The heat surge within waned, and I collapsed to the ground. I lay there a long time. The evening air cooled my body. My breath slowed. A canopy of barren branches was silhouetted against the darkening sky. Time passed, and I became empty. Without thought. Without feeling. There was only that moment.

My body shivered, and I was aware of the rolling thunder in me. Turning onto my back, I opened my arms and legs to the night sky. My mouth widened, and a long low wail flowed from the recesses of my body. The moist air swelled the sound, and it echoed back to me from the shadow of the barn. The ground billowed around me, and I slipped deep into Earth's fold, cradled in my darkest hour.

• • •

"I'm a worn-out woman," I say to my therapist. I say that to Nancy too. And to Steve. Sometimes even to the children.

I've cried a lot this past year. Mostly at night to Nancy when the others are asleep. I also cry when I walk. On winter mornings before work on the Nordic-Track in our basement. Swish. Swish. Swish. The tears come, and sometimes anguished sobs. I wonder if John hears me through the thin wall that separates me from his bedroom. I also walk during lunch hour at the newspaper. And in the evenings around the three-mile loop near our home. Past neighbors' houses and farmers' fields. In my pocket is the CD player Nancy gave me. I turn the volume high and sing out loud. Half way around the loop I lie in the tall grass at the edge of a field. Feet splayed, arms open wide. Dusk hides me from passing cars. The ground is moist, cool. Like the night on the hill behind our house. The Earth comforts me. Strength seeps in from powers beyond my knowing.

Lying there, I hear again the therapist's words: "What do you want from your relationship with Steve?" She and I use to talk about the changes going on within the family; now we talk mostly about my anger. And how not to become bitter. It's either or, she says. You get better or you become bitter.

"I'm a single mother with four children," I tell her. "He's like another child. Worse. I can control them. But not him."

Then I tell her of my dream: Steve and I are with family and friends. We're outside. Maybe at a picnic or a high school graduation party. Everything appears normal, like it often does. Suddenly it comes to me. I can't do this anymore. It's too hard; I will crack. In my dream I tell Steve that I'm leaving him. I see his face. He's shocked and angry. But mostly afraid. The people at the party say it's okay, that they understand. Steve hurls soup at me. Warm and sticky, it drips from my body. I remain firm. I can't do this. It's not about *becoming* bitter, I say to the therapist. I already am.

• • •

John is home from the hockey game. His team won. We eat potato soup and open-faced salami and cheese sandwiches. A makeshift meal from my childhood. Mom was adept at these kinds of meals. She liked to tell of how she could have potato soup ready to serve her family in fifteen minutes. I'm also a resourceful cook. Easy, quick, and nutritious meals. After dinner, I pack school lunches. Check homework. Sign a permission slip for a field trip. Darkness settles on us, and Elly asks again when Daddy will be home. I say I don't know but that he will be okay. I say that often, as if hearing the words will make it true. He needs to be by himself for a while, I say, and then I rub her back and stroke her fine blond hair. I remind her to breathe deeply. When her breath evens, I go to my own bed but do not sleep.

Shortly before midnight I hear the sound of wheels on gravel. He is home. He parks far from the house, hoping I won't know that he has returned. I don't hear the front door open, but I do hear footsteps as he creeps downs the stairs to his office. I know by these things that he's not okay. That it's not over yet. He's safe for now, though. Worry ebbs, and I slip into a restless sleep.

Several days later, after the acute stage of the episode passes, Steve writes extensively about what happened while he was away. His writings cover ten single-spaced pages of a yellow legal pad. They reveal a mind slipping over the edge. At the top of the first page, he prints: "These are notes on my <u>over-reaction</u> to Linda's words on March 18, at 10 a.m. till Tuesday, March 20, at approximately 5:00 a.m. During this time, I drive myself out of state and out of their lives." Below are excerpts of his writing.

> Sunday, 10 a.m.: Linda's words send me.
> 10:01: Linda tells me she's going to dinner with Mary Ann without me. I look dis-

appointed/hurt. She says
I can have dinner with her
some other night. I say will
you go with me? She says,
No, without any hesitation.
Immediately I feel enraged. I
don't want to talk, I want to
be gone.

10:05 a.m.: Linda goes to get
Elly from religion class. I take
the opportunity and leave the
house and drive back roads
very slowly into upstate New
York. I return home 13 hours
and 10 minutes later via I-79
because it's dark and safer
(than taking the back roads).
After 411 miles and never
turning the radio on, I'm
frustrated still, but at 11:30
Sunday night, I sneak into
the office. I get zero sleep that
night. I hear Linda above me
stirring all night, except for a
period between 1-2:30 a.m.

Monday Morn.: "They" wake
up and leave. No contact. I'm
awake but speak to no one.
I stay in the office until 9:30
a.m. Then I get up with manic
energy and quickly prepare
for a long trip to New Orleans
and possibly on Interstate

10 to California if things get really bad between us. I pack food, drinks, cooler, gallon of milk, tools, note pad, approximately $300 cash and credit cards, medication, shorts, etc. Since I saw snow on the ground in northern Pennsylvania and New York the first day, I decided to go south; I could better sleep in the car with warm coveralls, pillow, blanket, three pairs of socks and a tassel cap...Took snow tires off and changed the oil before I left. Got a Rambler oil filter for the next oil change. Jiffy Lube may not have one...

When I go, I leave signs so they think of me and know that I'm not there:
• I parked one of the Ramblers crossways blocking the door. The front bumper was almost touching the front step. This made use of the front door very difficult. Also, Linda will have to think of something to tell anyone who stops over. I put a note in the windshield that said, "miss me." Locked the car so that it stayed put; took both sets of keys. I left notes throughout

the house. Some nice. But one very clear, where I told Linda to give up her private talks with Mary Ann.
• I hid the cordless phone. And took two phones off the hook, but made them look like they were on (the hook).
• Turned off the surge protector for our computer.
• Left dog out and intentionally didn't tie her.
• Left a note that I loved Elly.

• If Linda still wanted to see Mary Ann, she would have found all four of our cars disabled. If she did not give up her scheming, she probably would have started missing work. Power to the house may have gone off. No lights. No well water. No flush. Hopefully it wouldn't take too many days for her to realize it's not a good idea to keep things from your spouse...But I do love her.

During an episode, Steve's mind swings between extremes. One of the notes I found reads, "Enjoy the warm weather." The one under my bed pillow wasn't so sweet: "If you really do still love me, you will not have dinner with Mary Ann and while she's in Pittsburgh, you will not see her for lunch, have her over, or talk on the phone ... Call to cancel dinner, but that's it. Hang up. Don't answer if she calls you back... I'm going to want some straight answers when I get home."

Steve also wrote about being angry with Luke for not listening to him when he tries to help fix his dirt bike, and at me, for not supporting what he wants. And he talked about his frustrations at not being able to discipline the children: "I don't have enough confidence to tell the kids what to do. I ask them to do something, not tell them. ... If Linda wants them to do something, it will probably happen. But I'm not Linda."

• • •

Steve doesn't make it to New Orleans the second day; he only drives about three hundred miles from home, to southern West Virginia. As the mania subsides, he calls me. He's hesitant, still slightly suspicious, but I hear a change in his voice. The fact that he's calling tells me he's getting better. I beg him to come home, and eventually he agrees to.

Shortly before dawn, I hear the Rambler wheels on our graveled driveway; this time he comes down the hill and onto the cement pad. I hear the car door slam and the front door open, and my breath deepens in relief. He's unguarded as he moves freely about the house. Moments later he's in the bedroom undressing. I stay where I am, for I want to say or do nothing that will set him off. When he crawls into bed, he's distant, unapologetic. In his notes, he wrote of his return: "I told her that I loved her, but couldn't touch, hold, or kiss her."

He exhales deeply, and I know the demons are retreating and the unnerving events of the past forty-four hours are coming to a close. It's an hour before dawn, and I'm exhausted. A worn out woman. I will get up soon and leave for work, utterly spent by another sleepless night.

• • •

The fallout from these episodes resonates through our life for several months. The paranoia and manic energy that prompted his leave-taking are gone, but his mental faculties are compromised. He is less capable of remembering where he's supposed to be or what he's supposed to do. He can't concentrate sufficiently to read a newspaper or magazine. Last week he bought parts for a car that didn't need fixing. I write in my journal several weeks after this episode: "Steve's inability to perform is so pronounced again. The heat pump blower has been out for 10 days, and temperatures dipped to 16 degrees. The replacement motor sits at the top of the steps, but he's unable to follow through with any task. It took three phone calls before he got the right car part for his Rambler. He's embarrassed and ashamed, not trusting himself or his mind to be there for him."

Six weeks later, I added, "He's still more irritable than usual. And he's spending money we don't have. He's very talkative and a little wild. When he and I met for lunch, he went over the line when talking to the woman at the next table."

Usually socially astute—not a given for many engineers—Steve is less able to read people's behaviors when interacting with others following an episode. After this particular one, he talked frequently about Cleopatra, an out-of-the-blue fixation that he repeatedly interjected into the conversation when we hosted card club at our house several weeks after he came back. Why Cleopatra? I don't know. After everyone left, I told him I really didn't want to hear about her anymore, and the Egyptian Queen faded from his banter.

Steve's willingness to share details about these episodes—where he went and what he thought—helped me learn how to deal with them. It took a very long time for me to understand an episode for what it was, and not as something that Steve could control. When they first occurred, I tried reasoning with him, hoping he could understand his faulty thought processes. With experience and education, though, I came to accept—or at least not challenge—that sometimes he perceived situations differently than others did. With time I learned to pull back and let an episode play itself out and, most importantly, never to try to stop him.

Steve's episodes didn't occur often, but they increased in frequency as his mind deteriorated. They finally stopped after he again began taking the antipsychotic Risperdal. Only one has occurred since then.

It was while we were at Rice Lake, a fishing camp two hours northeast of Toronto where Steve and his family have vacationed since he was seven. The first time I went was the summer before we were married. Through the years other family and friends joined the Schmitmeyers for this biennial getaway: Nancy and her family, the Clunes and their three children, Bob and Mary Ann and their family, Steve's sister, Joyce, and her family, and a college friend and her kids. Very dear people who'd supported us steadfastly through these difficult years.

Antipsychotic medication is sedating and has myriad side effects; especially worrisome is that long-term use can cause involuntary body movement, called tardive dyskinesia. After Steve had been on the drug for several years, his psychiatrist suggested he try not taking it. Steve's psychosis had lingered for almost three years following the episode in Detroit, but the psychiatrist speculated that it may not be chronic, only a residual side effect of the initial breakdown. Over a period of six months the doctor slowly decreased the dosage; six months after he stopped taking the drug, he had an episode.

The trigger was a disagreement with his father. We'd been at Rice Lake for several days when Steve and his father decided to take their small fishing boat to a nearby marina because the motor wasn't running right. John, in college by then, went with them. After they pulled the boat from the water, Steve stooped between the car and boat to hook up the safety chains. Steve's father dismissed his effort, telling Steve that the chains weren't necessary for such a short trip. Then he motioned John to pull the car forward. When John did, he nearly knocked his father over.

Steve said nothing at the time, but when he got back from the marina, left without telling anyone.

His leaving triggered my usual anxiety. What if someone tried to stop him? Could he navigate these less familiar back roads? And where would he stay when he came back? At our house he always retreated to the office, but there was very little privacy in the cabin.

Despite the worry, I knew what needed to be done for his eventual return. Nancy suggested the boys stay in her cabin that night and Elly sleep in my bed. This would give Steve a place to go when he returned. I left a note for him, and, on the hunch that he would probably leave again the next day, even packed a lunch for him to take. He returned around midnight, after everyone was in bed, and left before sunup. Later, on the second afternoon, he came back, the mania having subsided. As usual, we talked about what happened. It was then that he told me that he thought about not coming back, worried that I would take the car keys so he couldn't leave again.

"I wouldn't do that," I said. "Once, maybe. But not anymore."

"If the keys were gone I planned to drown myself in the lake," he said. I sighed at hearing his confession. It's important to know these things but not easy to hear them. "My plan was to go to the middle of the lake and tie the anchor to my legs. I'd cut the anchor rope so no one would find me," he said.

I shuttered, unnerved by what didn't happen.

Steve smiled, grabbing my knee in his familiar gesture of endearment.

"But you didn't take them," he said, his voice brimming with gratitude. "And you even packed a lunch for me to take."

I've read a lot about living with someone who has a mental illness, but there is nothing in the literature that tells you how to react at times like this. The ability to respond prudently comes from remaining open to new ways of thinking about the workings of our minds, and learning from the previous episodes. Steve's willingness to share such dark secrets deepened my understanding. His sharing also helped keep him safe.

Chapter 15

Finding a New Normal

A cameraman from a Pittsburgh TV station walks backwards up the hill from our barn. He pivots left to pan the back yard and pasture then turns his camera on Steve, John, Elly, and me, who walk slowly from the barn to the house. Steve is carrying a pumpkin I grew in our garden. Behind us is our century-old barn. It was one of the reasons we decided to buy a newer home, instead of older farmhouses like we had in Ohio. The barn had been moved to the property by the previous owner and made our place feel more farm-like. The barn sits atop an old stone foundation and is an idyllic backdrop for a TV news story about bipolar research at the Stanley Center.

A year has passed since Steve be-

gan taking Risperdal, and he's been re-
markably stable since then. He doesn't
talk about SAE any more, and his ability
to think clearly has improved. Most importantly, he hasn't had another episode.
Now he and our family are being featured
in a television clip as an example of the
successes being achieved through research at the Stanley Center. During the
broadcast, the reporter encourages "the
one in a hundred people who suffer from
bipolar disorder" to become part of the
center's patient registry, through which
their illnesses will be tracked and treated.

"We have a real opportunity here
in Pittsburgh to do something absolutely
unique about a devastating illness," says
one of the co-investigators interviewed for
the segment.

Following our walk to the house,
the cameraman films us on the deck
carving a jack-o-lantern. He zooms in on
Steve as he shapes the mouth while nine-
year-old Elly looks on. John, home on fall
break from his first year as an engineering student at the University of Dayton, is
seen scooping the gourd's gooey innards

into the old truck hubcap we use for com-
post. Luke, who didn't want to be on TV,
watches from a distance. Later, Steve and
I sit with the reporter at the picnic table
discussing the challenges families face
when living with a severe mental illness.

"I said, 'Wow! Why is this happening?'" Steve says to the reporter about
when he first experienced sharp mood
swings. "I just had no idea."

"Confusion. Chaos. Uncertainty," I
add. "You're on solid ground...and then,
all of a sudden, you're blindsided."

The reporter thanks our family on
camera and says we are courageous for
talking about an illness many people don't
think is real. Then he tells the viewers:
"The Schmitmeyers are now rebuilding
their lives with a better understanding
of bipolar disorder. With medication and
psychotherapy, researchers say bipolar
patients like Steve can lead fully function-
al normal lives."

The decision to participate in the
segment about mental illness wasn't
simple, for it meant going public on a subject that, for the most part, we didn't talk

openly about. Very few people were privy to the periodic upheavals in our home. Most—casual friends, country neighbors, and the parents of our children's friends who we sat beside at hockey games and school open houses—were unaware of the severity of Steve's condition. A few knew that Steve and I had separated and he'd been hospitalized several years earlier. "Exhaustion," I'd said then. "He'd been through a difficult time with work and needs to be away for a while." And since no additional details emerged over the years, these casual friends probably assumed that we'd patched over our differences and life had returned to normal. The people I worked with at the newspaper also didn't know. Certainly my fellow journalists would be surprised seeing my family featured in a TV segment about mental illness.

Bipolar and schizoaffective disorders are complex and extremely difficult diagnoses to understand. They don't have biological markers, which would make them easier for people to accept. And because the symptoms are mercurial and af-

fect personality, it's awkward to talk openly about them. It never feels okay to speak
of a loved one's odd or erratic behaviors.
It's also why the stigma about these illnesses runs deep. Our involvement in
NAMI workshops and support groups had
been instrumental in helping us understand these disorders, and attending the
NAMI convention in Albuquerque was
pivotal in our talking more openly about
Steve's illness.

Stigma often stems from insufficient
or inaccurate information. In the mid-
1990s, the medical community's understanding of mental illness was evolving.
Even some of the literature NAMI distrib-
uted about mental illnesses was wrong.
While Steve was at St. Rita's, I'd visited
a local NAMI chapter's office to learn as
much as I could about his new diagnosis. I'd heard of bipolar disorder but knew
almost nothing about it. One of the brochures dealt with how mental illnesses
often occurs in people who have over-
protective mothers, a psychological con-
nection that lingered long after researchers debunked the theory. These kinds

of faulty messages contribute to stigma.
Brain research gained significant momentum in the 1990s, and to highlight its
importance, President George H. W. Bush
designated it The Decade of the Brain.
Scientists would delve deeper into brain
issues ranging from Alzheimer's to mental illness. Bush's declaration resulted in
more funding for the National Institute of
Health and the National Institute of Mental Health, but research is slow to affect
how people think about mental illness.
Eliminating stigma happens on a personal
level.

Although Steve and I were okay
with being more open about his illness,
we were sensitive to the repercussions it
might have for the children. After I talked
to them about going on TV, John and Elly
agreed to participate. Their ages, nineteen and nine, may have made it easier
for them to say yes, but fourteen-year-
old Luke didn't want to be on camera. He
didn't mind our doing so, he said. He just
didn't want to participate.

A hint of the repercussions about
our decision to go public became evident

even before the TV crew left that day. As the cameraman packed his gear, I approached him to say thanks for making the hour-long drive to our house. Kneeling on the cement pad outside our home, he was packing his equipment into a large duffel bag. Looking up, he acknowledged my comment, and then asked about why Luke didn't want to be on TV.

"He's fourteen," I said. "No one wants to be different from their friends at that age."

He shrugged, seemingly satisfied with the explanation and returned to what he was doing. But that wasn't the whole picture, for I knew that accepting Steve's mental illness had been challenging for Luke. I added, "It's been more difficult for him to understand his father's illness. Being a teenager isn't easy, and having mental illness in the family doesn't make it any easier."

"I don't get it either," the cameraman said, shaking his head, seemingly wanting to say more. Then he added, "I don't know. It doesn't seem real to me either."

I was taken aback that the cameraman so openly expressed his opinion. He
seemed somewhat detached throughout
the hour-long photo shoot and interview,
but I also knew that it wasn't his job to
engage us in conversation. I'd worked with
photographers at the newspaper, and they
generally kept their distance while the
reporter interacted with the people. But
I didn't want him to have the last word,
and tartly added, "I guess that's why we
agreed to do the interview. So people better understand how mental illnesses can
affect ordinary people."

The cameraman's words made me
bristle, for I knew how deeply our family
had been affected by Steve's illness. I also
knew how hard we'd worked to reclaim
a semblance of the life we had. Mental
illness is real. It nearly wrecked our family. And our agreeing to go public about
what happened seemed the beginning of
me wanting to tell our family's story, so
people like the cameraman would better
understand. Several weeks later, after the
segment aired on TV, I wrote in my journal, "It's a strain to maintain a 'normal'

life in a society that still considers mental illness a weakness... If people only knew what it was like. The roller coaster ride of the past four years cannot be told in a four-minute clip."

Steve's new combination of medications—lithium to stabilize his mood, Wellbutrin to counteract the depression, and an antipsychotic to suppress delusional and obsessive thoughts—was truly a milestone for Steve and our family. The changes in him didn't happen quickly, for regaining mental stability takes time. Slowly I began to trust the subtle, positive differences I saw. He could follow a conversation better. We could disagree about something without him shutting down. He no longer saw the ceiling move or heard music that wasn't there. He felt steadier descending the stairs. His obsessiveness diminished. And, most importantly, SAE no longer mattered. After years of ups and downs, the contented, easy-going man I married was back. Greatly changed, yes, but much more like the person he used to be.

The summer before the TV interview

aired, a couple invited us to a picnic at
their dock on the Allegheny River to celebrate John's graduation from high school.
John had worked as a gardener for them
for several years, and they knew he liked
to water ski. We got to the river around
four in the afternoon, and the kids and I
took turns skiing behind their boat. After
stopping for a picnic lunch on the shore,
the husband said there was time for a few
more runs before sunset. Both boys took
another turn. Then Steve said he wanted
to ski, something he hadn't done in years.

Steve had experienced numerous
physical changes since the onset of his
mental health problems. His body was
more rigid from the antipsychotic medication, and his ability to move confidently
through space was compromised. He lumbered more, in part because he was thirty
pounds heavier. Weight gain is one of the
many side effects of psychotropic drugs.
As a result, Steve was less physically active. His wanting to ski surprised me.

I stood on the bank watching Steve
put on the skis. Most people start in the
water because it's easier, but Steve al-

ways liked taking off from the dock so he could begin and end a run without getting his swimming suit wet, a feat he boasted about as a teenager. As the boat pulled him to standing position, I saw how intensely he focused on what he was doing. He stayed behind the boat for a long time, and then cautiously began zigzagging across the water. Tears welled in my eyes as I watched; seeing him ski, I felt a sense of hopefulness that I hadn't felt for a very long time.

There are no words to describe the relief I felt as Steve emerged from the shadow of his disorder. But it was a measured returned. With his diagnosis changed to schizoaffective, we slowly came to understand that his disability was permanent, that he would never return to the "fully functioning normal life" the co-investigator had implied during the TV interview. Although Steve was mentally stable and our family life less chaotic, his cognitive deficits remain. He's still challenged by planning, abstract thinking, mental inflexibility, and impulse control, brain functions permanently impaired by

the chemical imbalance—or by the concussion he sustained on the BMX track so
many years ago. He's stable, though, and
in many ways, himself again.

On the day the Pittsburgh TV segment aired, Steve applied for a job as-
sembling bicycles at a local retail store
for the Christmas season. We both knew
by then that he wouldn't work as an engineer again, but he wanted desperately
to do something. When he told me about
the job, I was thrilled that he was actively
looking for work again. Sales at Plasquip
had fizzled to almost nothing more than a
year ago, in part because of his illness but
also because a lot of the plastic injection
molding industry had moved overseas.

After my initial euphoria of hearing
that he was looking for a job, I was saddened by his search. Once so technically
astute, he was hoping to earn money putting together bicycles. "When will it stop
hurting," I wrote in my journal. "Why does
every step towards regaining a normal life
have to be a reminder of what has been
lost?"

Steve didn't get that job, but several

weeks later, a local Sears store hired him to work part-time in the hardware department. The Sears job served as a springboard back into living a life in which he actively participated and enjoyed. And like before, the people he worked with loved him. He tackled the job with the same interest and work ethic he'd had as an engineer, and with the same resolve he'd shown in overcoming his mental disorder.

"If I couldn't do this job," he said on the day he got his first Sears paycheck, "I can't imagine how I would have lived the rest of my life."

Chapter 16

A Silent Sadness

"I have a mind like an insect," Steve says as we come to the end of a walking trail that loops through a park near our home. Steve's voice is matter-of-fact, his face without expression, but I see the sag in his shoulders. Maybe he's tired from climbing the steep grade that leads to the parking lot. Or maybe he's sad because his mind isn't what he wants it to be.

It's a spring day many years later, and Steve and I walk frequently now that I no longer work full-time. Several years after the television interview—when the children were older and family life suf-ficiently stable for me to be away from home for longer periods—I took a job in public relations at the University of Pittsburgh, an hour-long commute from our home. I was at Pitt for twelve years, until accepting an early retirement package when I was sixty-three. The Pitt job was extremely valuable in stabilizing our family's finances. In addition to initially doubling my salary at the newspaper, it included tuition benefits, with which Luke and Elly earned their undergraduate degrees. My new job had better health-care coverage and a superb matching plan for rebuilding our retirement fund. The job allowed us to move closer to the standard of living we enjoyed prior to Steve's health problems. I still work part-time, as a freelance writer and editor for university alumni magazines. I also teach writing part-time at a university in Pittsburgh.

We live in the same house but think more about moving to a smaller one now that the children are grown. John, in his late-thirties now, lives in Cleveland, Ohio. He graduated from the University of Dayton and works as a mechanical engineer at an industrial hose manufacturing plant there. He and his wife, Suzie, named our first grandchild, George Simon, in part for my father, George Anthony Kerber.

Luke lives several miles from us. He's also a mechanical engineer; he works at a metal-coating company nearby. Luke got his father a job at the shop; the technical environment is ideal for Steve, who works part-time. Steve stayed at Sears for about seven years, but the increasing computerization was difficult for him. Then he drove for an auto-parts store. At first he had trouble getting the right part to the right shop and was put on probation twice. But he persevered, eventually developing a system that allowed him to avoid mistakes. But the experience was an eye-opener as to the kind of work Steve could do. He's had mild anxiety since the onset of his illness, especially with time-sensitive matters, which made delivering car parts too stressful.

Elly, in her late twenties, lives in western North Carolina. After earning her undergraduate degree in rehabilitation sciences—with a minor in art—she received a clinical doctorate degree in physical therapy and works at the Indian Hospital in Cherokee.

It feels especially good being outside in early spring. Sammie, also a Jack Russell Terrier, is with us. Our dog Spot died five years after Steve brought her home with him from St. Rita's. She liked chasing the boys on their dirt bikes and darted into the path of one and was killed instantly. Spot holds a special place in all of our hearts and is buried alongside the children's other pets at the edge of our woods.

As Steve and I crest the hill at the end of our walk, we stop at one of the two benches near the top to rest and watch the sun set. Steve's face glistens from the climb, and he removes his glasses and places them next to him on the bench, then wipes the sweat around his eyes. Sammie barks suddenly, a sharp, high-pitched sound that breaks the evening quiet. She's the first to spot a pair of Australian shepherds ascending the hill towards us.

"Let's go," I say. "I don't want to deal with any more dogs."

No bigger than a large cat, Sammie thinks she can take on any dog. She was especially aggressive today, her first long walk of the season. We stand quickly and head to the parking lot. When Steve remembers his glasses, he heads back to where we were sitting. Moments later I see him searching the ground around the wrong bench.

"There they are," I yell, trying not to get too close to the approaching shepherds.

The momentary distraction causes me to relax my grip on Sammie's leash, and she bolts for the two dogs. Running after her, I clamp my foot on the leash handle and apologize to the dogs' owner, who hurries by.

Steve, with his glasses on, is beside me now, and we walk towards the car. That's when he likens his mind to that of an insect's.

"What makes you say that?" I ask. It's been more than twenty years since the onset of Steve's mental health problems, and both of us better understand and accept the multitude of changes that have occurred in our life.

"I once read about wasps that live in the ground and lay their eggs by the hole leading to their nest. If you move the egg to the other side of the hole, the wasp will keep looking in the spot where the egg was. It never thinks to look elsewhere, and the egg dies," Steve says. "I'm like that wasp. When something doesn't work, I don't think of trying something different."

• • •

It is almost impossible to comprehend the kinds of challenges Steve faced as he worked his way back from a disorder that affects the mind. He hates being less capable than he once was, especially when doing things that were second nature. Like hooking up battery cables wrong. Or forgetting to add new oil after draining the old. That happened once when he was changing oil in the Fergie. He remembered that he didn't add the new oil after driving a short distance down the road. He immediately shut off the engine and called me to help tow the tractor home. One of our neighbors was outside when I got there. She wanted to know if Steve needed any help. He didn't tell her what happened, and she and I visited while he hooked up the tow strap to my car. When we got home he said, "I'm glad you didn't say anything to her about what I did. It's embarrassing."

Bipolar screw-ups. That what Steve calls the myriad blunders that continue to occur. But despite these setbacks, he doesn't retreat behind his disorder by letting others do what he can. Slowly and methodically, he does simpler projects, checking and re-checking himself every step of the way: Unclogging the kitchen sink drain. Changing the filter on the pipe that leads from the well to the house. Replacing worn wall sockets. Installing brake pads on a car.

Because Luke lives nearby, he sometimes works on his own car at our house, alongside Steve. Luke keeps a watchful eye on whatever Steve is working on, making sure he doesn't forget a critical step. But Luke also seeks his father's advice with whatever he's working on. My heart swells when I hear John or Luke consult their father about a technical problem, for despite his limitations, he has a wealth of technical knowledge that the boys frequently tap into. In his late sixties now, he's reluctant to take on his own car or home repair projects, but he enjoys helping his children with whatever task they are doing.

He's also joined a club that collects antique outboard boat motors. He has several from the 1950s, simpler two-stroke engines that he keeps in good working order. And he has a '58 garden tractor that he takes to farm shows. Although tempered by age and circumstance, Steve's zeal for living is robust. What is different in these twilight years is the understanding he has of life's darker side, something that eluded him when we sat together on the front steps of my house in college so many years ago.

Steve was in his late forties when his mind stabilized, and he faced the challenge of finding a way forward different from what his life had been. It was also different from how his friends lived their lives. He had to reimagine life not as the engineer he always wanted to be but as a laborer working part-time. He also had to learn to be okay with frequent input from me on the many choices he makes each day, and to live a more regulated life, for he knows how stimuli can tax a beleaguered mind. That means leaving a party early to get the sleep necessary for maintaining good mental health. And not driving in the passing lane to minimize the visual onslaught of cars coming at you. "I don't trust my reflexes to be as quick as they once were," he said when I asked why. It also means stepping away from John and Suzie's wedding reception to sit in a car by himself, so he can celebrate later into the night. There were other places at the reception where Steve could relax, but he still favors being in a car.

"Our dad doesn't use drive-throughs anymore," Elly once told one of my brothers as he pulled into McDonalds for a cup of coffee. Seeing my brother's confusion, I explained: "Too much stimuli; it makes it harder for him to think." That's something I notice in ways I hadn't before, how noise bombards us doing simple things like using a drive-through. The crackle of the intercom, the loud scratchy voice of the person taking your order, the back-and-forth of placing an order. It's taxing, so Steve always orders his coffee inside.

Living a well-regulated life also means resting his mind for extended periods every day. Steve begins most days sitting for several hours in his favorite chair, in part to emerge from the sedating effect of Risperdal, which he takes in the evening. He also sits there after work and when he wants a mental break from whatever he's doing. It isn't necessarily from a difficult task, but from simpler jobs too, like vacuuming the floors. Whether it's the noise from the sweeper or the constancy of having to use his mind, he often takes breaks. Sometimes he reads, mostly technical magazines and newspapers, but also automotive books, like *Wheels for the World*, a history of the Ford Motor Company. He especially likes true-to-life stories about individuals overcoming great odds, like Jeannette Walls' *Glass Castle* or Laura Hillenbrand's *Unbroken*. He's a voracious reader now, something he rarely did before he was sick. It's likely where he learned about the wasp that failed to look elsewhere for its egg.

Sometimes I'll find him staring blankly into space, his recliner pushed back so that he's parallel with the floor.

"What are you thinking about?" I ask as I pass.

"Nothing," he says.

"How can you not think about something?" I say.

"I don't know," he responds with a smile. "I'm resting my mind."

What began in the early years of his recovery as an ordinary reclining chair amid the other furniture in our living room has evolved into a thoughtfully arranged haven in a corner. Around him is everything he needs: a coaster for his morning coffee or evening beer; a calendar, a clock, a radio; scissors and a stapler; pen, pencils, paper, and Post-It notes; technical reference books; the slide rule he used in college; a spreadsheet to track a set of exercises Elly made for him; and an endless supply of reading material. Atop the small radio is a miniature

John Deere tractor and trailer, similar to the full-size tractors he hauled from Ohio. And hanging on the wall behind the recliner is a large framed photograph of the dairy farm where he grew up. Life was simpler then, but not necessarily any happier than now. There's often newspaper and magazine articles he's clipped to share circling the recliner.

"One. Two. Three. Four. Five. Six. Seven. Eight," I say as I count the piles around the chair. I still hate clutter and periodically remind him that he has reached the limit of what I can tolerate. The next time I pass through he'll have consolidated the stacks into neat little piles.

Steve's reliance on his recliner as a place to re-center his mind is indicative of the understanding we both have about maintaining good mental health. To be sure, I continue to play an active role in keeping Steve stable, for he relies on me to recognize changes in him that might signal abnormal shifts in his mood. Medication significantly lessens mood swings, but they don't go away. Sometimes I see the change in Steve's glassy, unfocused eyes. Mostly I hear it in his voice. Flat when he's low, faster and louder when swinging high. There's also sharpness to his laugh when his mind leans to manic, a harsher and less natural sound than the normal robust laughter that is his trademark. I'm still his mental governor, for although Steve understands these changes as symptoms of his illness, he's less skilled at seeing them in himself. His strength is in his willingness to trust me and to accept these subtle signs for what they are. People don't like being told that they're laughing too loud, but Steve listens with an equanimity few could muster.

Steve's ability to be the positive, upbeat person he once was speaks to the heart of who he is. Throughout his illness, he's had an intuitive sense of how to care for himself. An avowed non-writer—or at least one more adept at technical prose—Steve tracked his thoughts, behaviors, moods, and feelings for several years in an attempt to understand what was happening. These data points offered insight into how his mind functioned, sometimes even before the psychiatrist understood what was happening. In a data point written two years after his breakdown, Steve noted that he was able to read electrical drawings while on an antipsychotic drug, which he took for several months following his hospitalization. His mental instability remained until a psychiatrist reintroduced the medication three years after Detroit.

Even when in the throes of an episode, Steve had an innate sense of how to care for himself. When mania flared, he would leave home and drive for hours until his mind quieted. He returned only when he was on the road to recovery, when he intuitively knew his mind could deal with whatever it was that prompted him to leave in the first place. He also took steps to ensure his safety while on the road by openly acknowledging what few are willingly to admit. "I'M BIPOLAR," he wrote in large block letters on the front page of the small calendar he carried in his pocket. A similar note protruded from one of the card slots in his wallet, should someone confront him while on the road. He took these precautions when his mind was balanced, for he knew they might protect him when it wasn't.

Most importantly, Steve trusted me with deeply intimate thoughts most people would be too ashamed to share. Keeping a viable pathway of communication between us helped me understand what he was going through. I learned a great deal by remaining open and learning all I could from NAMI workshops and conferences, but Steve's willingness to share his troubled thoughts was key in helping me keep him safe.

Mental illness often strikes younger people, those in the throes of becoming who they are. The average age for the onset of bipolar disorder is early- to mid-twenties; Steve was in his early forties. If Steve had any advantage in regaining the life he wanted, it was in knowing who he was before he got sick. More mature then, he also was better able to accept that he could no longer navigate the world as he once did.

"I don't know who I'll be when this

is over," he'd said after his walk with Elly
along the rocky banks of the creek. To
be robbed of your sense of self is something few can imagine. It also hints to the
breadth and depth of his journey as he
made his way back to a meaningful life.

● ● ●

Although I appreciate the magni-
tude of Steve's struggle, being in a marriage with a man whose ongoing health
concerns are an integral part of the relationship isn't easy. In my early fifties
when a semblance of our earlier life began
to return, I had to re-imagine my life being with a man whose health needs were
at the forefront of our life together. And
with a partner who wasn't fully aware of
the depth of his own loss. "I want to live
again," I told my therapist, whom I continued to see occasionally for another five or
six years after Steve's mood stabilized. "I
don't want my whole life to revolve around
caring for a sick husband."

Steve may again be upbeat and
easy-going, but he isn't able to engage

in life as he once did. He wasn't able to commiserate with me to the extent most husbands can over issues concerning the children, nor wrestle with financial matters, such as retirement. He is less capable of analyzing the pros and cons of issues, or even comprehending the depth of his diminished abilities.

"I have the illusion of a life partner," I said to the therapist as I struggled to find my way forward, "not someone who is there when I need him." With Steve less able to be involved in dealing with day-to-day problems, I had to accept and be okay with reaching out to others with concerns most couples face together. Many have been there for me, filling voids left vacant by what happened. Nancy, foremost, but also her husband, Mark. When trying to decide whether to take an early retirement offer from Pitt, I talked mostly with Mark, whom I continue to consult about financial and other matters in which Steve used to actively participate. And I often turn to our close friends, who understand Steve's limitations and are always ready to help.

There are also our adult children,
who grew up in close proximity to the
perplexing symptoms of Steve's disorder.
I talked often and openly about the symptoms of their father's illness, and, as a
result, they engaged early on in scrutiniz-
ing their own mental health. When they
were younger, the three of them visited
my therapist a couple of times, who always ensured me they were "coping well
under the circumstances." And as teenagers, Luke and Elly joined a longitudinal
research study for children with a bipolar
parent. John, in his early twenties when
the National Institute of Mental Health
funded the first phase of the study, was
too old to participate. The study involves
blood draws, annually filling out a lengthy
questionnaire, and an in-person interview every other year in an effort to track
people at high risk for mental illnesses.
They are still part of the study, and Luke,
in his mid-thirties now, is thought to be
the oldest participating offspring. This
early scrutiny has made them more aware
of their own mental health, as well as of
Steve's and my well-being. Thinking back

to those difficult years, when I worried how the children would fare, I know now that they are better adjusted to life's ups and downs for having been part of our family's challenge. Today they live engaging, productive, and fun-loving lives, separate from ours, yet part of a family constellation linked closely to Steve and me, and to each other.

• • •

"I think we share more than the average family," Luke says as we sit together in the living room talking about the impact of their father's illness on their lives. John, Luke, and Elly are home for a long holiday weekend. I'm nearing the end of this writing project and have asked them to share their perspective on growing up with a father who has a mental illness. Our sitting together in the living room is reminiscent of earlier family meetings, but now they participate willingly, over gin and tonics and an array of cheeses John's wife, Suzie, brought for our weekend together. As we talk, our toddler grandson plays with the red wooden truck Steve made when John was born. Suzie has known our family for more than a decade. The youngest of five siblings, she lost her mother when she was twelve. "Many families face adversity," she said of our family's challenge, "but what is different about your experience is how openly and honestly you talk about what happened."

When I ask how they live their lives differently because of the experience, John says he's more tolerant of other people's behaviors. "There are a lot of people in the shop where I work who have rough lives, but I don't judge them. I'm willing to work around their problems to get a job done."

"I especially feel for the homeless," says Elly. "I think I'm much more empathetic toward them than I would have been otherwise." Her brothers nod in agreement.

"I know I'm less concerned with what others think and more okay with being who I am," says Luke. Laughter erupts at his comment, for of the three, Luke lives the most non-conventional lifestyle.

He continues: "I think I'm more open to things because of it. I was so wrong in my thinking about Pop's illness. You really can't know what another person is going through unless you experience it."

For almost an hour their conversation rambles freely, from their embarrassment about our family's financially strapped lifestyle to their pride in the unique and adventuresome way our family plays together; from their learning how not to sweat the small stuff to a heightened awareness of what it might mean to bind your life to another's.

"I better understand the huge commitment involved in saying yes to a relationship," says Elly, who's been dating a young man she met in graduate school. He's visiting our home for the first time over the holiday weekend. "It's really unknown as to what you're signing on for."

John, Luke, and Elly also talk about being in tune with their own emotional and psychological needs.

"Playing hard is an important part of my adult life," says John.

"I try not to let my life get too far

out of balance," says Luke.

"I feel validated to pull back and not participate in something if it feels too much for me," says Elly.

Despite their busy adult lives, all three remain aware of different aspects of Steve's and my life. Luke on a more regular basis, because he lives near us. But also John and Elly, who pay attention from afar. When Steve is ordering new tires for one of the cars, John is quick to do the research and pass on his recommendations. And Elly calls frequently to check in, and, as a physical therapist, to monitor our exercise habits. She reminds us frequently of staying physically active as we age. But she also knows how much I enjoy our long, rambling phone conversations. Sometimes we cook together via FaceTime, she in her North Carolina kitchen and me in my Pennsylvania home, the hours slipping away as we chat.

When I ask if they feel more responsible for our well-being than their peers might feel towards their parents, tears well in Elly's eyes. "You both made a commitment to our family," she says. "I don't feel that being committed to you and our family's well-being is my responsibility, but more so something I want to do."

• • •

Our family's experience with mental illness strengthened each of us in ways I could never have foreseen. Although I still experience feelings of loss, a kind of silent sadness for the husband who once was, living with Steve's disorder has taught me to engage fully in living every day, for I have seen what it's like when that's no longer possible.

I once sought a grander life, one I'd imagined from the books I read as a child. But my life journey took me inward, towards a better understanding of self. It's given me a greater appreciation for the resiliency of the human spirit. When thoughts of *what if* emerge, I move into the moment, toward humility, for there I am at peace with what is.

Epilogue

Whoosh. Whoosh. Whoosh. That's the sound of bicycle wheels on the rain-soaked trail leading into Washington, D.C. It was the seventh day of our bike trip—Steve's, Nancy's, and mine—and it had been raining steadily for two hours.

We began the day's ride a few miles south of Harper's Ferry, about fifty miles from D.C. It drizzled all morning, then turned to a downpour. Being wet wasn't the worst part though; it was our tires flinging coarse gravelly sand from the trail upward, clogging our gears and slipping into our saddlebags. Clinging to our calves and lower backs and settling into the spouts of our water bottles. Grit was everywhere, but we pedaled on. When we reached the end, Nancy's husband, Mark, was there with dry towels in hand. He'd covered the car seats with sheets of plastic for the trip to our friend's house, where we stayed. The next day, we loaded our bikes and equipment onto Mark's van and headed home, three hundred and fifty-five miles from where we started.

Nancy and I have been biking together for ten years. We still live far from each other, she and Mark in northern Illinois and Steve and I in western Pennsylvania. But each year in late spring the two of us ride for a week along the converted railroad trails that spider through Pennsylvania, Ohio, Virginia, Maryland, and West Virginia. Steve, Mark, and others have joined us for all or parts of these bike trips, but mostly it's been Nancy and me covering two to three hundred miles in a week.

Then Steve said he wanted to bike from Pittsburgh to D.C. It was an ambitious goal, since he hadn't done much long-distance biking in years. Even though we've walked regularly since I no longer work full time, bicycling is different. It requires more mental energy, and the sustained concentration could be fatiguing. Still, Steve wanted to try.

"We'll call it our anniversary ride,"

I said as we finalized plans for a trip the following spring. "Some people take exotic vacations when they're married forty years. We'll ride our bikes to D.C." And in light of Nancy's significance in our life, it seemed natural that she be part of the journey.

The bicycle trail between Pittsburgh and D.C. is really two trails, the C&O Canal and Great Allegheny Passage. The GAP trail begins in Pittsburgh, where the Allegheny and Monongahela rivers meet, then follows the Youghiogheny and Casselman rivers through the Allegheny Mountains into Cumberland, Maryland. From there, the C&O trail snakes alongside the Potomac to Georgetown, where the trail ends. Nancy and I have biked parts of these two trails several times during our years of riding, but we never rode them from beginning to end in a week.

It was sunny and clear the morning we left Pittsburgh. Standing in front of the water fountain where the Allegheny and Monongahela rivers converge, we snapped lots of pictures. First Nancy and Mark, then Steve and me. Next, the four of us.

And finally Steve, Nancy, and me with our bicycles, spray from the fountain flashing against a brilliant blue sky.

It's not easy to explain the bond that's formed among the four of us through the years. Life's challenges, both the Bokermanns and ours, cemented an intimacy that anchors our alliance. A quiet closeness unimaginable when Nancy and I warmed ourselves by the fire barrel at the University of Dayton as we watched Steve skate. Sisterly love, yes, but a connectedness that transcends understanding. Though we our separated by hundreds of miles, there is a synchronization to our lives that is beyond explanation. It is there in our perceptions and beliefs, our views and our values. But also in the way we reach for our phones at the same time to call one another. And in the similar clothes we inadvertently wear when together. All six of our now-grown children roll their eyes when they see Nancy and me in our matching blue bathrobes carrying our coffee cups towards each other's cabin at Rice Lake in the morning.

Shortly after Steve emerged from

the most difficult phase of his illness, I
began thinking about documenting the
knotty challenges a family faces when
a loved one is diagnosed with a serious
mental disorder. I created a timeline of
events beginning with Steve walking into
the kitchen and telling me he'd quit his
job, to a decade later, when he said he'd
drown himself in Rice Lake if I interfered
with his leaving. Near the end of the docu-
ment, a novella in itself, I wrote of Nancy's
role in helping me face those challenges:

> Sometimes I would call Nancy
> and sob so deeply it took my
> breath away. I would put a
> pillow to my face so the kids
> wouldn't hear and let the pain
> in me rise to the surface and
> pour out. It had to have been
> difficult for her to listen to
> me. But she always did. She
> was never too busy, and she
> never judged my actions or
> me. She was also a mother to
> my children when I couldn't
> be. And she cradled me in my
> misery, despite the miles that
> separated us.

Recapturing a meaningful, consequential life after a family member is diagnosed with a life-changing mental illness involves the support of countless other people, and in that our family was fortunate. There were many who held us during those dark days in ways too numerous to remember.

But I also had the advantage of inheriting the strength and determination of those who came before. It was there in the way my parents lived their lives. Through their example, they endowed me with the potential to push through and persevere, and for that I am grateful. And that inner strength transcends generations. As a young woman, Liwwät Böke crossed the ocean alone to start her family. Her grit allowed her to overcome unimaginable hardships. Through it all she documented daily life in the wilderness so that "my children's children will come to read my writings ... and will better understand who they are..."

Mental illness is a devastating diagnosis, but it isn't insurmountable—if the many resources necessary to transcend the challenge are within reach.

Our bike trip began in late May in near-perfect weather. Temperatures were in the mid-70s, and light breezes blew off the rivers. On the second day, as we began the gradual climb toward the Eastern Continental Divide, it turned hot and muggy. It took us two days to reach the divide, which forms the Gulf of Mexico and Atlantic Seaboard watersheds. When we reached the summit, we rested briefly on Big Savage Mountain, where on a clear day there is a breathtaking view of the rolling mountains of Pennsylvania, West Virginia, and Maryland. But dark rain clouds blocked our view the day we were there. And during the twenty-mile descent into Cumberland, it poured. When we got to our hotel, Mark was waiting with towels to dry off and beers to toast another day's ride.

Slowly the miles slipped away, through the rutted, muddy trail east of Cumberland and past the canal's teeming aquatic wildlife and historic Fort Frederick and Harper's Ferry. Finally, we were on the packed, sandy trail leading into D.C.

Fourteen miles upstream from the capital is Great Falls, Virginia, where the Potomac narrows to create a series of waterfalls. It's usually a popular and picturesque layover for people using the trail, but few were around the rainy afternoon we stopped on the bridge above the rushing waters to take a selfie. Together Steve, Nancy, and I stood above the rapids, three silver-haired bikers in rain-soaked slickers. Stretching out my arm, I clicked the camera. There we were, still smiling, and reveling in our shared accomplishment. We were going to make it all the way.

In Gratitude

It takes a village. That notion was never far from my thoughts as I wrote *Rambler*. It took the concerted effort of many to overcome the odds of recapturing a family life rerouted by severe mental illness. The same is true for this book. Many played a part.

Foremost among them is my brother, Bob Kerber, a steadfast champion from the beginning. When I first sat before the mound of paperwork generated by my husband's illness—our personal writings, psychiatrists' notes that spanned a decade, police and FBI reports, informational brochures from the National Alliance on Mental Illness—I talked frequently with Bob about organizing and structuring the details of our experience. More importantly, we discussed the voice with which I would tell such an intimate, delicate story.

After one conversation, Bob sent an email reminding me that writing about Steve's illness would mean plumbing the depths of my being, for I would again face the pain and fears associated with those challenging years. He concluded with, "If you can do this, I will help you in any way that I can." He wrote that more than a dozen years ago, and his enthusiasm and support have never wavered. Among his many contributions is reading every word of every iteration of this book several times over.

I also want to thank my readers: Mary Ann Borch, Cynthia Gill, Gail Oare, Eleanor Schmitmeyer, Suzie Schmitmeyer, Juliana Taymans, and John Thorndike. Their insight and suggestions helped hone the story and make *Rambler* a better read.

I want to acknowledge the contributions of The Artists' Orchard's Steve Hallock for his precise and comprehensive editing and publisher Sherry Kaier for her commitment to producing a top-notch publication and for her thoughtful and gentle encouragement throughout the process. I also want to recognize the expertise and professionalism of Peter Brunetto of Brunetto Design for creating *Rambler's* eye-catching book cover.

There are countless people—family and friends, coworkers and fellow writers—whose faith in my writing helped me believe that one day this book would happen. Most important among them is my family—my husband, Steve, and my children: John and his wife, Suzie; Luke; and Eleanor. They've been my most enthusiastic supporters, and their willingness to allow such a forthright telling of our family's personal challenge never wavered. They are my joy. And my sister, Nancy Bokermann, whose support and caring are beyond measure.

Rambler: A Family Pushes Through the Fog of Mental Illness is the manifestation of so much that is good in my life. It is the repository of the positive energy and love that flowed from this life-altering experience.

Linda K. Schmitmeyer

is a freelance writer and editor and adjunct university instructor. Formerly a high school English teacher, beat reporter, features editor, and public relations professional, she wrote a newspaper column for years about the everyday adventures of parenting with her car-centric husband, Steve. Now she blogs about her experience with caring for a husband with a mental illness when her children were young. You can follow her on Twitter @LKSchm and visit her blog at www.lindaschmitmeyer.com. She and Steve live in western Pennsylvania.